AUTUMN LIGHT

AUTUMN LIGHT

Illuminations of Age

L. M. SCHULMAN, *Editor*

THOMAS Y. CROWELL NEW YORK

AUTUMN LIGHT: Illuminations of Age
Copyright © 1978 by Lester Martin Schulman
For information address Thomas Y. Crowell, 10 East 53 Street,
New York, N. Y. 10022. Published simultaneously in Canada by
Fitzhenry & Whiteside Limited, Toronto.
Designed by Patricia Parcell

Library of Congress Cataloging in Publication Data
Main entry under title: Autumn light.
CONTENTS: McCullers, C. The sojourner.—Angell, R.
Tennis.—Capote, T. Miriam. [etc.]
1. Short stories, American. 2. Aging—Fiction.
[1. Old age—Fiction. 2. Short stories.]
I. McCullers, Carson Smith, 1917–1967. II. Schulman, L. M.
PZ1.A93 [PS648.A37] [Fic.] 77–26582 ISBN 0–690–03885–2
First Edition

Acknowledgments

The author and publisher gratefully acknowledge permission granted to use:

"A Clean, Well-Lighted Place" by Ernest Hemingway, reprinted from *Winner Take Nothing* with the permission of Charles Scribner's Sons. Copyright 1933 Charles Scribner's Sons.

"A Forgotten Poet" from *Nabokov's Dozen* by Vladimir Nabokov. Copyright 1944 by Atlantic Monthly Company. Reprinted by permission of Doubleday & Company, Inc.

"The Home Front" reprinted with the permission of Farrar, Straus & Giroux, Inc. from *Children Are Bored on Sunday* by Jean Stafford, Copyright 1945 by Jean Stafford, renewed Copyright © 1972 by Jean Stafford.

CONTENTS

PREFACE

Spin a coin on a tabletop. Watch it as the spinning slows, the blur of motion like mist dissolving, the shape, the design, the value emerging. Before it falls.

Take this as an image of aging. And you will begin to see how the writers in this volume have put the theme to use in these ten tales.

Writers of fiction have only the characters they create to transmit their vision of human existence. Each of these stories has at its center a person growing old, and through that process moving into achingly sharp focus. No better agent could be found to convey the vision that has spurred the author into art.

In "The Sojourner," the hero's awakening to age becomes a recognition of his human solitude and need for love—twin dilemmas that lie at the heart of Carson

McCullers' work. Roger Angell, noted for the extraordinary depth of his sports reportage, employs his sense of sports as a touchstone of life in a story that turns tennis into a contest of man against time. The obsession with the malevolent outsider harbored by Truman Capote attains eerie embodiment in his "Miriam"; Jean Stafford's sensitivity to individual lives trapped in the currents of history finds perfect lodging in "The Home Front"; Hortense Calisher's feeling for the depths of horror beneath the surface of middle-class gentility echoes in "The Scream on Fifty-Seventh Street"; Ernest Hemingway's commitment to grace and courage in the face of forces that can never be defeated gives his "A Clean, Well-Lighted Place" its heroic dimension. We see Vladimir Nabokov's mocking contempt for inane official authority and his appreciation of subterranean and subversive desire in "A Forgotten Poet," while Kurt Vonnegut, Jr.'s blending of science-fiction imagination and social concern produces the nightmare-come-true of "Tomorrow and Tomorrow and Tomorrow." Jean Rhys's loathing of the junglelike savagery that she has come to identify with the journey through life reaches a peak of intensity in "Sleep It Off, Lady"—an intensity that takes on a haunting poignancy as she looks back on the lost paradise of childhood in "I Used to Live Here Once," the remarkable cameo that ends the journey where it began—and fittingly closes this collection.

In these stories, then, you will discover aging to be a final statement, both of the lives of the characters and of the message that each author feels driven to send the reader throughout a creative lifetime. Even more, you may gain an intimation of its place and power in your own life as well, as you move from a life with a future to a life with a past, and from hopes and dreams to ultimate illumination of the truth that your life has exposed.

L. M. Schulman

AUTUMN LIGHT

THE SOJOURNER

Carson McCullers

T HE TWILIGHT BORDER between sleep and waking was a Roman one this morning; splashing fountains and arched, narrow streets, the golden lavish city of blossoms and age-soft stone. Sometimes in this semi-consciousness he sojourned again in Paris, or German war rubble, or Swiss skiing and a snow hotel. Sometimes, also, in a fallow Georgia field at hunting dawn. Rome it was this morning in the yearless region of dreams.

John Ferris awoke in a room in a New York hotel. He had the feeling that something unpleasant was awaiting him—what it was, he did not know. The feeling, submerged by matinal necessities, lingered even after he had dressed and gone downstairs. It was a cloudless autumn day and the pale sunlight sliced between the pastel sky-scrapers. Ferris went into the next-door drugstore and sat at the end booth next to the window glass that over-looked the sidewalk. He ordered an American breakfast with scrambled eggs and sausage.

Ferris had come from Paris to his father's funeral which had taken place the week before in his home town in Georgia. The shock of death had made him aware of youth already passed. His hair was receding and the veins in his now naked temples were pulsing and prominent and his body was spare except for an incipient belly bulge. Ferris had loved his father and the bond between them had once been extraordinarily close—but the years had somehow unraveled this filial devotion; the death, expected for a long time, had left him with an unforeseen dismay. He had stayed as long as possible to be near his mother and brothers at home. His plane for Paris was to leave the next morning.

Ferris pulled out his address book to verify a number. He turned the pages with growing attentiveness. Names and addresses from New York, the capitals of Europe, a few faint ones from his home state in the South. Faded, printed names, sprawled drunken ones. Betty Wills: a random love, married now. Charlie Williams: wounded in the Hürtgen Forest, unheard of since. Grand old Williams—did he live or die? Don Walker: a B.T.O. in television, getting rich. Henry Green: hit the skids after the war, in a sanitarium now, they say. Cozie Hall: he had heard that she was dead. Heedless, laughing Cozie—it was strange to think that she too, silly girl, could die. As Ferris closed the address book, he suffered a sense of hazard, transience, almost of fear.

It was then that his body jerked suddenly. He was staring out of the window when there, on the sidewalk, passing by, was his ex-wife. Elizabeth passed quite close to him, walking slowly. He could not understand the wild quiver of his heart, nor the following sense of recklessness and grace that lingered after she was gone.

Quickly Ferris paid his check and rushed out to the sidewalk. Elizabeth stood on the corner waiting to cross Fifth Avenue. He hurried toward her meaning to speak, but the lights changed and she crossed the street before he reached her. Ferris followed. On the other side he could easily have overtaken her, but he found himself lagging unaccountably. Her fair brown hair was plainly rolled, and as he watched her Ferris recalled that once his father had remarked that Elizabeth had a "beautiful carriage." She turned at the next corner and Ferris followed, although by now his intention to overtake her had disappeared. Ferris questioned the bodily disturbance that the sight of Elizabeth aroused in him, the dampness of his hands, the hard heart-strokes.

It was eight years since Ferris had last seen his ex-wife.

He knew that long ago she had married again. And there were children. During recent years he had seldom thought of her. But at first, after the divorce, the loss had almost destroyed him. Then after the anodyne of time, he had loved again, and then again. Jeannine, she was now. Certainly his love for his ex-wife was long since past. So why the unhinged body, the shaken mind? He knew only that his clouded heart was oddly dissonant with the sunny, candid autumn day. Ferris wheeled suddenly and, walking with long strides, almost running, hurried back to the hotel.

Ferris poured himself a drink, although it was not yet eleven o'clock. He sprawled out in an armchair like a man exhausted, nursing his glass of bourbon and water. He had a full day ahead of him as he was leaving by plane the next morning for Paris. He checked over his obligations: take luggage to Air France, lunch with his boss, buy shoes and an overcoat. And something—wasn't there something else? Ferris finished his drink and opened the telephone directory.

His decision to call his ex-wife was impulsive. The number was under Bailey, the husband's name, and he called before he had much time for self-debate. He and Elizabeth had exchanged cards at Christmastime, and Ferris had sent a carving set when he received the announcement of her wedding. There was no reason *not* to call. But as he waited, listening to the ring at the other end, misgiving fretted him.

Elizabeth answered; her familiar voice was a fresh shock to him. Twice he had to repeat his name, but when he was identified, she sounded glad. He explained he was only in town for that day. They had a theater engagement, she said—but she wondered if he would come by for an early dinner. Ferris said he would be delighted.

As he went from one engagement to another, he was still bothered at odd moments by the feeling that something necessary was forgotten. Ferris bathed and changed in the late afternoon, often thinking about Jeannine: he would be with her the following night. "Jeannine," he would say, "I happened to run into my ex-wife when I was in New York. Had dinner with her. And her husband, of course. It was strange seeing her after all these years."

Elizabeth lived in the East Fifties, and as Ferris taxied uptown he glimpsed at intersections the lingering sunset, but by the time he reached his destination it was already autumn dark. The place was a building with a marquee and a doorman, and the apartment was on the seventh floor.

"Come in, Mr. Ferris."

Braced for Elizabeth or even the unimagined husband, Ferris was astonished by the freckled red-haired child; he had known of the children, but his mind had failed somehow to acknowledge them. Surprise made him step back awkwardly.

"This is our apartment," the child said politely.

"Aren't you Mr. Ferris? I'm Billy. Come in."

In the living room beyond the hall, the husband provided another surprise; he too had not been acknowledged emotionally. Bailey was a lumbering red-haired man with a deliberate manner. He rose and extended a welcoming hand.

"I'm Bill Bailey. Glad to see you. Elizabeth will be in, in a minute. She's finishing dressing."

The last words struck a gliding series of vibrations, memories of the other years. Fair Elizabeth, rosy and naked before her bath. Half-dressed before the mirror of her dressing table, brushing her fine, chestnut hair. Sweet, casual intimacy, the soft-fleshed loveliness indisputably possessed. Ferris shrank from the unbidden memories and compelled himself to meet Bill Bailey's gaze.

"Billy, will you please bring that tray of drinks from the kitchen table?"

The child obeyed promptly, and when he was gone Ferris remarked conversationally, "Fine boy you have there."

"We think so."

Flat silence until the child returned with a tray of glasses and a cocktail shaker of Martinis. With the priming drinks they pumped up conversation: Russia, they spoke of, and the New York rain-making, and the apartment situation in Manhattan and Paris.

"Mr. Ferris is flying all the way across the ocean tomorrow," Bailey said to the little boy who was perched on the arm of his chair, quiet and well behaved. "I bet you would like to be a stowaway in his suitcase."

Billy pushed back his limp bangs. "I want to fly in an airplane and be a newspaperman like Mr. Ferris." He added with sudden assurance, "That's what I would like to do when I am big."

Bailey said, "I thought you wanted to be a doctor."

"I do!" said Billy. "I would like to be both. I want to be a atom-bomb scientist too."

Elizabeth came in carrying in her arms a baby girl. "Oh, John!" she said. She settled the baby in the father's lap. "It's grand to see you. I'm awfully glad you could come."

The little girl sat demurely on Bailey's knees. She wore a pale pink crêpe de Chine frock, smocked around the yoke with rose, and a matching silk hair ribbon tying back her pale soft curls. Her skin was summer tanned and her brown eyes flecked with gold and laughing. When she reached up and fingered her father's horn-rimmed glasses, he took them off and let her look through them a moment. "How's my old Candy?"

Elizabeth was very beautiful, more beautiful perhaps than he had ever realized. Her straight clean hair was shining. Her face was softer, glowing and serene. It was a madonna loveliness, dependent on the family ambiance.

"You've hardly changed at all," Elizabeth said, "but it has been a long time."

"Eight years." His hand touched his thinning hair self-consciously while further amenities were exchanged.

Ferris felt himself suddenly a spectator—an interloper among these Baileys. Why had he come? He suffered. His own life seemed so solitary, a fragile column supporting nothing amidst the wreckage of the years. He felt he could not bear much longer to stay in the family room.

He glanced at his watch. "You're going to the theater?"

"It's a shame," Elizabeth said, "but we've had this engagement for more than a month. But surely, John, you'll be staying home one of these days before long. You're not going to be an expatriate, are you?"

"Expatriate," Ferris repeated. "I don't much like the word."

"What's a better word?" she asked.

He thought for a moment. "Sojourner might do."

Ferris glanced again at his watch, and again Elizabeth apologized. "If only we had known ahead of time—"

"I just had this day in town. I came home unexpectedly. You see, Papa died last week."

"Papa Ferris is dead?"

"Yes, at Johns Hopkins. He had been sick there nearly a year. The funeral was down home in Georgia."

"Oh, I'm so sorry, John. Papa Ferris was always one of my favorite people."

The little boy moved from behind the chair so that he

could look into his mother's face. He asked, "Who is dead?"

Ferris was oblivious to apprehension; he was thinking of his father's death. He saw again the outstretched body on the quilted silk within the coffin. The corpse flesh was bizarrely rouged and the familiar hands lay massive and joined above a spread of funeral roses. The memory closed and Ferris awakened to Elizabeth's calm voice.

"Mr. Ferris' father, Billy. A really grand person. Somebody you didn't know."

"But why did you call him *Papa* Ferris?"

Bailey and Elizabeth exchanged a trapped look. It was Bailey who answered the questioning child. "A long time ago," he said, "your mother and Mr. Ferris were once married. Before you were born—a long time ago."

"Mr. Ferris?"

The little boy stared at Ferris, amazed and unbelieving. And Ferris' eyes, as he returned the gaze, were somehow unbelieving too. Was it indeed true that at one time he had called this stranger, Elizabeth, Little Butterduck during nights of love, that they had lived together, shared perhaps a thousand days and nights and—finally—endured in the misery of sudden solitude the fiber by fiber (jealousy, alcohol and money quarrels) destruction of the fabric of married love.

Bailey said to the children, "It's somebody's suppertime. Come on now."

"But Daddy! Mama and Mr. Ferris—I—"

Billy's everlasting eyes—perplexed and with a glim-
mer of hostility—reminded Ferris of the gaze of another
child. It was the young son of Jeannine—a boy of seven
with a shadowed little face and knobby knees whom
Ferris avoided and usually forgot.

"Quick march!" Bailey gently turned Billy toward the
door. "Say good night now, son."

"Good night, Mr. Ferris." He added resentfully, "I
thought I was staying up for the cake."

"You can come in afterward for the cake," Elizabeth
said. "Run along now with Daddy for your supper."

Ferris and Elizabeth were alone. The weight of the
situation descended on those first moments of silence.
Ferris asked permission to pour himself another drink
and Elizabeth set the cocktail shaker on the table at his
side. He looked at the grand piano and noticed the music
on the rack.

"Do you still play as beautifully as you used to?"

"I still enjoy it."

"Please play, Elizabeth."

Elizabeth arose immediately. Her readiness to perform
when asked had always been one of her amiabilities; she
never hung back, apologized. Now as she approached
the piano there was the added readiness of relief.

She began with a Bach prelude and fugue. The prelude
was as gaily iridescent as a prism in a morning room. The
first voice of the fugue, an announcement pure and soli-

tary, was repeated intermingling with a second voice, and again repeated within an elaborated frame, the multiple music, horizontal and serene, flowed with unhurried majesty. The principal melody was woven with two other voices, embellished with countless ingenuities—now dominant, again submerged, it had the sublimity of a single thing that does not fear surrender to the whole. Toward the end, the density of the material gathered for the last enriched insistence on the dominant first motif and with a chorded final statement the fugue ended. Ferris rested his head on the chair back and closed his eyes. In the following silence a clear, high voice came from the room down the hall.

"Daddy, how *could* Mama and Mr. Ferris—" A door was closed.

The piano began again—what was this music? Unplaced, familiar, the limpid melody had lain a long while dormant in his heart. Now it spoke to him of another time, another place—it was the music Elizabeth used to play. The delicate air summoned a wilderness of memory. Ferris was lost in the riot of past longings, conflicts, ambivalent desires. Strange that the music, catalyst for this tumultuous anarchy, was so serene and clear. The singing melody was broken off by the appearance of the maid.

"Miz Bailey, dinner is out on the table now."

Even after Ferris was seated at the table between his

host and hostess, the unfinished music still overcast his mood. He was a little drunk.

"L'improvisation de la vie humaine," he said. "There's nothing that makes you so aware of the improvisation of human existence as a song unfinished. Or an old address book."

"Address book?" repeated Bailey. Then he stopped, noncommittal and polite.

"You're still the same old boy, Johnny," Elizabeth said with a trace of the old tenderness.

It was a Southern dinner that evening, and the dishes were his old favorites. They had fried chicken and corn pudding and rich, glazed candied sweet potatoes. During the meal Elizabeth kept alive a conversation when the silences were overlong. And it came about that Ferris was led to speak of Jeannine.

"I first knew Jeannine last autumn—about this time of the year—in Italy. She's a singer and she had an engagement in Rome. I expect we will be married soon."

The words seemed so true, inevitable, that Ferris did not at first acknowledge to himself the lie. He and Jeannine had never in that year spoken of marriage. And indeed, she was still married—to a White Russian money-changer in Paris from whom she had been separated for five years. But it was too late to correct the lie. Already Elizabeth was saying: "This really makes me glad to know. Congratulations, Johnny."

He tried to make amends with truth. "The Roman autumn is so beautiful. Balmy and blossoming." He added, "Jeannine has a little boy of six. A curious trilingual little fellow. We go to the Tuileries sometimes."

A lie again. He had taken the boy once to the gardens. The sallow foreign child in shorts that bared his spindly legs had sailed his boat in the concrete pond and ridden the pony. The child had wanted to go in to the puppet show. But there was not time, for Ferris had an engagement at the Scribe Hotel. He had promised they would go to the guignol another afternoon. Only once had he taken Valentin to the Tuileries.

There was a stir. The maid brought in a white-frosted cake with pink candles. The children entered in their night clothes. Ferris still did not understand.

"Happy birthday, John," Elizabeth said. "Blow out the candles."

Ferris recognized his birthday date. The candles blew out lingeringly and there was the smell of burning wax. Ferris was thirty-eight years old. The veins in his temples darkened and pulsed visibly.

"It's time you started for the theater."

Ferris thanked Elizabeth for the birthday dinner and said the appropriate good-byes. The whole family saw him to the door.

A high, thin moon shone above the jagged, dark skyscrapers. The streets were windy, cold. Ferris hurried to

Third Avenue and hailed a cab. He gazed at the noctur-
nal city with the deliberate attentiveness of departure and
perhaps farewell. He was alone. He longed for flighttime
and the coming journey.

The next day he looked down on the city from the air,
burnished in sunlight, toylike, precise. Then America
was left behind and there was only the Atlantic and the
distant European shore. The ocean was milky pale and
placid beneath the clouds. Ferris dozed most of the day.
Toward dark he was thinking of Elizabeth and the visit
of the previous evening. He thought of Elizabeth among
her family with longing, gentle envy and inexplicable
regret. He sought the melody, the unfinished air, that
had so moved him. The cadence, some unrelated tones,
were all that remained; the melody itself evaded him. He
had found instead the first voice of the fugue that Elizabeth had played—it came to him, inverted mockingly
and in a minor key. Suspended above the ocean the
anxieties of transience and solitude no longer troubled
him and he thought of his father's death with equanimity.
During the dinner hour the plane reached the shore of
France.

At midnight Ferris was in a taxi crossing Paris. It was
a clouded night and mist wreathed the lights of the Place
de la Concorde. The midnight bistros gleamed on the
wet pavements. As always after a transocean flight the
change of continents was too sudden. New York at

morning, this midnight Paris. Ferris glimpsed the disorder of his life: the succession of cities, of transitory loves; and time, the sinister glissando of the years, time always.

"Vite! Vite!" he called in terror. *"Dépêchez-vous."*

Valentin opened the door to him. The little boy wore pajamas and an outgrown red robe. His grey eyes were shadowed and, as Ferris passed into the flat, they flickered momentarily.

"J'attends Maman."

Jeannine was singing in a night club. She would not be home before another hour. Valentin returned to a drawing, squatting with his crayons over the paper on the floor. Ferris looked down at the drawing—it was a banjo player with notes and wavy lines inside a comic-strip balloon.

"We will go again to the Tuileries."

The child looked up and Ferris drew him closer to his knees. The melody, the unfinished music that Elizabeth had played, came to him suddenly. Unsought, the load of memory jettisoned—this time bringing only recognition and sudden joy.

"Monsieur Jean," the child said, "did you see him?"

Confused, Ferris thought only of another child—the freckled, family-loved boy. "See who, Valentin?"

"Your dead papa in Georgia." The child added, "Was he okay?"

Ferris spoke with rapid urgency: "We will go often to the Tuileries. Ride the pony and we will go into the guignol. We will see the puppet show and never be in a hurry any more."

"Monsieur Jean," Valentin said. "The guignol is now closed."

Again, the terror, the acknowledgment of wasted years and death. Valentin, responsive and confident, still nestled in his arms. His cheek touched the soft cheek and felt the brush of the delicate eyelashes. With inner desperation he pressed the child close—as though an emotion as protean as his love could dominate the pulse of time.

TENNIS
Roger Angell

T HE THING YOU ought to know about my father is that he plays a lovely game of tennis. Or rather, he used to, up to last year, when all of a sudden he had to give the game up for good. But even last summer, when he was fifty-five years of age, his game was something to see. He wasn't playing any of your middle-aged tennis, even then. None of that cute stuff, with lots of cuts and drop shots and getting everything back, that most older men play when they're beginning to carry a little fat and don't like to run so much. That wasn't for him. He still played all or nothing—the big game with a hard serve and coming right in behind it to the net. Lots of running in that kind of game, but he could still do it. Of course, he'd begun to make more errors in the last few years and that would annoy the hell out of him. But still he wouldn't change—not him. At that, his game was something to see when he was on. Everybody talked about it. There was always quite a little crowd around his court on the weekends, and when he and the other men would come off the court after a set of doubles, the wives would see their husbands all red and puffing. And then they'd look at my old man and see him grinning and not even breathing hard after *he'd* been doing all the running back after the lobs and putting away those overheads, and they'd say to him, "Honestly, Hugh, I just don't see how you do it, not at your age. It's *amaz*ing! I'm going to take my Steve [or Bill or Tom] off cigarettes and put him on a diet. He's ten years younger and just look at him." Then my old man would light up a cigarette and smile and shake his head and say, "Well, you know how it is. I just play a lot." And then a minute later he'd look around at everybody lying on the lawn there in the sun and pick out me or one of the other younger fellows and say, "Feel like a set of singles?"

If you know north Jersey at all, chances are you know my father. He's Hugh Minot—the Montclair one, not the fellow out in New Brunswick. Just about the biggest realty man in the whole section, I guess. He and my mother have this place in Montclair, thirty-five acres, with a swimming pool and a big vegetable garden and this En-Tout-Cas court. A lovely home. My father got a little name for himself playing football at Rutgers, and that helped him when he went into business, I guess. He never played tennis in college, but after getting out he wanted something to sort of fill in for the football— something he could do well, or do better than the next man. You know how people are. So he took the game up. Of course, I was too little to remember his tennis game when he was still young, but friends of his have told me that it was really hot. He picked the game up like nothing at all, and a couple of pros told him if he'd only started earlier he might have gotten up there in the big time— maybe even with a national ranking, like No. 18 or so. Anyhow, he kept playing and I guess in the last twenty years there hasn't been a season where he missed more than a couple of weekends of tennis in the summertime. A few years back, he even joined one of these fancy clubs in New York with indoor courts, and he'd take a couple of days off from work and go in there just so that he could play in the wintertime. Once, I remember, he played doubles in there with Alice Marble and I think Sidney Wood. He told my mother about that game lots of times, but it didn't mean much to her. She used to play tennis years ago, just for fun, but she wasn't too good and gave it up. Now the garden is the big thing with her, and she hardly ever comes out to their court, even to watch.

I play a game of tennis just like my father's. Oh, not as good. Not nearly as good, because I haven't had the experience. But it's the same game, really. I've had people tell me that when they saw us playing together—that we both made the same shot the same way. Maybe my backhand was a little better (when it was on), and I used to think that my old man didn't get down low enough on a soft return to his forehand. But mostly we played the same game. Which isn't surprising, seeing that he taught me the game. He started way back when I was about nine or ten. He used to spend whole mornings with me, teaching me a single shot. I guess it was good for me and he did teach me a good, all-round game, but even now I can remember that those morning lessons would somehow discourage both of us. I couldn't seem to learn fast enough to suit him, and he'd get upset and shout across at me, "Straight arm! Straight arm!" and then *I'd* get jumpy and do the shot even worse. We'd both be glad when the lesson ended.

I don't mean to say that he was so *much* better than I was. We got so we played pretty close a lot of the time. I can still remember the day I first beat him at singles. It was in June of 1937. I'd been playing quite a lot at school and this was my first weekend home after school ended. We went out in the morning, no one else there, and, as usual, he walked right through me the first set—about 6–1 or so. I played much worse than my regular game then, just like I always did against him for some reason. But the next set I aced him in the second game and that set me up and I went on and took him, 7–5. It was a wonderful set of tennis and I was right on top of the world when it ended. I remember running all the way back to the house to tell Mother about it. The old man came in and sort of smiled at her and said something like "Well, I guess I'm old now, Amy."

But don't get the idea I started beating him then. That was the whole trouble. There I was, fifteen, sixteen years old and getting my size, and I began to think, Well, it's about time you took him. He wasn't a young man any more. But he went right on beating me. Somehow I never played well against him and I knew it, and I'd start pressing and getting sore and of course my game would go blooey.

I remember one weekend when I was in college, a whole bunch of us drove down to Montclair in May for a weekend—my two roommates and three girls we knew. It was going to be a lot of fun. But then we went out for some tennis and of course my father was there. We all played some mixed doubles, just fooling around, and then he asked me if I wanted some singles. In that casual way of his. And of course it was 6–2, 6–3, or some such thing. The second set we were really hitting out against each other and the kids watching got real quiet, just as if it was Forest Hills. And then when we came off, Alice, my date, said something to me. About him, I mean. "I think your father is a remarkable man," she said. "Simply remarkable. Don't you think so?'' Maybe she wanted to make me feel better about losing, but it was a dumb question. What could I say except yes?

It was while I was in college that I began to play golf a little. I liked the game and I even bought clubs and took a couple of lessons. I broke ninety one day and wrote home to my father about it. He'd never played golf and he wrote back with some little gag about its being an old man's game. Just kidding, you know, and I guess I should have expected it, but I was embarrassed to talk about golf at home after that. I wasn't really very good at it, anyway.

I played some squash in college, too, and even made the B team, but I didn't try out for the tennis team. That disappointed my father, I think, because I wasn't any good at football, and I think he wanted to see me make some team. So he could come and see me play and tell his friends about it, I guess. Still, we did play squash a few times and I could beat him, though I saw that with time he probably would have caught up with me.

I don't want you to get the idea from this that I didn't have a good time playing tennis with him. I can remember the good days very well—lots of days where we'd played some doubles with friends or even a set of singles where my game was holding up or maybe even where I'd taken one set. Afterward we'd walk back together through the orchard, with my father knocking the green apples off the path with his racket the way he always did

and the two of us hot and sweaty while we smoked cigarettes and talked about lots of things. Then we'd sit on
the veranda and drink a can of beer before taking a dip
in the pool. We'd be very close then, I felt.

And I keep remembering a funny thing that happened
years ago—oh, away back when I was thirteen or four-
teen. We'd gone away, the three of us, for a month in
New Hampshire in the summer. We played a lot of
tennis that month and my game was coming along pretty
fast, but of course my father would beat me every single
time we played. Then he and I both entered the little
town championship there the last week in August. Of
course, I was put out in the first round (I was only a kid),
but my old man went on into the finals. There was quite
a big crowd that came to watch that day, and they had a
referee and everything. My father was playing a young
fellow—about twenty or twenty-one, I guess he was. I
remember that I sat by myself, right down beside the
court, to watch, and while they were warming up I
looked at this man playing my father and whispered to
myself, but almost out loud, "Take him! Take him!" I
don't know why, but I just wanted him to beat my father
in those finals, and it sort of scared me when I found that
out. I wanted him to give him a real shellacking. Then
they began to play and it was a very close match for a few
games. But this young fellow was good, really good. He
played a very controlled game, waiting for errors and

only hitting out for winners when it was a sure thing. And he went on and won the first set, and in the next my father began to hit into the net and it was pretty plain that it wasn't even going to be close in the second set. I kept watching and pretty soon I felt very funny sitting there. Then the man won a love game off my father and I began to shake. I jumped up and ran all the way up the road to our cabin and into my room and lay down on my bed and cried hard. I kept thinking how I'd wanted to have the man win, and I knew it was about the first time I'd ever seen my father lose a love game. I never felt so ashamed. Of course, that was years and years ago.

I don't think any of this would have bothered me except for one thing—I've always *liked* my father. Except for this game, we've always gotten along fine. He's never wanted a junior-partner son, either in his office or at home. No Judge Hardy stuff or "Let me light your cigar, sir." And no backslapping, either. There have been times where I didn't see much of him for a year or so, but when we got together (at a ball game, say, or during a long trip in a car), we've always found we could talk and argue and have a lot of laughs, too. When I came back on my last furlough before I went overseas during the war, I found that he'd chartered a sloop. The two of us went off for a week's cruise along the Maine coast, and it was swell. Early-morning swims and trying to cook over charcoal and the wonderful quiet that comes over those little coves after you've anchored for the night and the wind has dropped and perhaps you're getting ready to shake up some cocktails. One night there, when we were sitting on deck and smoking cigarettes in the dark, he told me something that he never even told my mother—that he'd tried to get into the Army and had been turned down. He just said it and we let it drop, but I've always been glad he told me. Somehow it made me feel better about going overseas.

Naturally, during the war I didn't play any tennis at all. And when I came back I got married and all, and I was older, so of course the game didn't mean as much to me. But still, the first weekend we played at my father's—the very first time I'd played him in four years—it was the same as ever. And I'd have sworn I had outgrown the damn thing. But Janet, my wife, had never seen me play the old man before and *she* spotted something. She came up to our room when I was changing afterward. "What's the matter with you?" she asked me. "Why does it mean so much to you? It's just a game, isn't it? I can see that it's a big thing for your father. That's why he plays so much and that's why he's so good at it. But why you?" She was half kidding, but I could see that it upset her. "This isn't a contest," she said. "We're not voting for Best Athlete in the County, are we?" I took her up on that and tried to explain the thing a little, but she wouldn't try to understand. "I just don't like a sore-head," she told me as she went out of the room.

I guess that brings me down to last summer and what happened. It was late in September, one of those wonderful weekends where it begins to get a little cool and the air is so bright. Father had played maybe six or seven sets of doubles Saturday, and then Sunday I came out with Janet, and he had his regular tennis gang there—Eddie Earnshaw and Mark O'Connor and that Mr. Lacy. I guess we men had played three sets of doubles, changing around, and we were sitting there catching our breath. I was waiting for Father to ask me for our singles. But he'd told me earlier that he hadn't been able to get much sleep the night before, so I'd decided that he was too tired for singles. Of course, I didn't even mention that out loud in front of the others—it would have embarrassed him. Then I looked around and noticed that my father was sitting in one of those canvas chairs instead of standing up, the way he usually did between sets. He looked awfully pale, even under his tan, and while I was looking at him he suddenly leaned over and grabbed his stomach and was sick on the grass. We all knew it was pretty bad, and we laid him down and put his cap over his eyes, and I ran back to the house to tell Mother and phone up the doctor. Father didn't say a word when we carried him into the house in the chair, and then Dr. Stockton came and said it was a heart attack and that Father had played his last game of tennis.

You would have thought after that and after all those months in bed that my father would just give up his tennis court—have it plowed over or let it go to grass. But Janet and I went out there for the weekend just last month and I was surprised to find that the court was in good shape, and Father said that he had asked the gang to come over, just so I could have some good men's doubles. He'd even had a chair set up in the orchard, halfway out to the court, so he could walk out there by himself. He walked out slow, the way he has to, and then sat down in the chair and rested for a couple of minutes, and then made it the rest of the way.

I haven't been playing much tennis this year, but I was really on my game there that day at my father's. I don't think I've ever played better on that court. I hardly made an error and I was relaxed and I felt good about my game. The others even spoke about how well I played.

But somehow it wasn't much fun. It just didn't seem like a real contest to me, and I didn't really care that I was holding my serve right along and winning my sets no matter who my partner was. Maybe for the first time in my life, I guess, I found out that it was only a game we were playing—only that and no more. And I began to realize what my old man and I had done to that game. All that time, all those years, I had only been trying to grow up and he had been trying to keep young, and we'd both done it on the tennis court. And now our struggle was over. I found that out that day, and when I did I suddenly wanted to tell my father about it. But then I looked over at him, sitting in a chair with a straw hat on his head, and I decided not to. I noticed that he didn't seem to be watching us at all. I had the feeling, instead, that he was *listening* to us play tennis and perhaps imagining a game to himself or remembering how he would play the point—the big, high-bouncing serve and the rush to the net for the volley, and then going back for the lob and looking up at it and the wonderful feeling as you uncoil on the smash and put the ball away.

MIRIAM

Truman Capote

F OR SEVERAL YEARS, Mrs. H. T. Miller had lived alone in a pleasant apartment (two rooms with kitchenette) in a remodeled brownstone near the East River. She was a widow: Mr. H. T. Miller had left a reasonable amount of insurance. Her interests were narrow, she had no friends to speak of, and she rarely journeyed farther than the corner grocery. The other people in the house never seemed to notice her: her clothes were matter-of-fact, her hair iron-gray, clipped and casually waved; she did not use cosmetics, her features were plain and inconspicuous, and on her last birthday she was sixty-one. Her activities were seldom spontaneous: she kept the two rooms immaculate, smoked an occasional cigarette, prepared her own meals and tended a canary.

Then she met Miriam. It was snowing that night. Mrs. Miller had finished drying the supper dishes and was thumbing through an afternoon paper when she saw an advertisement of a picture playing at a neighborhood theater. The title sounded good, so she struggled into her beaver coat, laced her galoshes and left the apartment, leaving one light burning in the foyer: she found nothing more disturbing than a sensation of darkness.

The snow was fine, falling gently, not yet making an impression on the pavement. The wind from the river cut only at street crossings. Mrs. Miller hurried, her head bowed, oblivious as a mole burrowing a blind path. She stopped at a drugstore and bought a package of pepper-mints.

A long line stretched in front of the box office; she took her place at the end. There would be (a tired voice groaned) a short wait for all seats. Mrs. Miller rummaged in her leather handbag till she collected exactly the cor-rect change for admission. The line seemed to be taking its own time and, looking around for some distraction, she suddenly became conscious of a little girl standing under the edge of the marquee.

Her hair was the longest and strangest Mrs. Miller had ever seen: absolutely silver-white, like an albino's. It flowed waist-length in smooth, loose lines. She was thin and fragilely constructed. There was a simple, special elegance in the way she stood with her thumbs in the pockets of a tailored plum-velvet coat.

Mrs. Miller felt oddly excited, and when the little girl glanced toward her, she smiled warmly. The little girl walked over and said, "Would you care to do me a favor?"

"I'd be glad to, if I can," said Mrs. Miller.

"Oh, it's quite easy. I merely want you to buy a ticket for me; they won't let me in otherwise. Here, I have the money." And gracefully she handed Mrs. Miller two dimes and a nickel.

They went into the theater together. An usherette directed them to a lounge; in twenty minutes the picture would be over.

"I feel just like a genuine criminal," said Mrs. Miller gaily, as she sat down. "I mean that sort of thing's against the law, isn't it? I do hope I haven't done the wrong thing. Your mother knows where you are, dear? I mean she does, doesn't she?"

The little girl said nothing. She unbuttoned her coat and folded it across her lap. Her dress underneath was prim and dark blue. A gold chain dangled about her neck, and her fingers, sensitive and musical-looking, toyed with it. Examining her more attentively, Mrs. Miller decided the truly distinctive feature was not her hair, but her eyes; they were hazel, steady, lacking any childlike quality whatsoever and, because of their size, seemed to consume her small face.

Mrs. Miller offered a peppermint. "What's your name, dear?"

"Miriam," she said, as though, in some curious way, it were information already familiar.

"Why, isn't that funny—my name's Miriam, too. And it's not a terribly common name either. Now, don't tell me your last name's Miller!"

"Just Miriam."

"But isn't that funny?"

"Moderately," said Miriam, and rolled the peppermint on her tongue.

Mrs. Miller flushed and shifted uncomfortably. "You have such a large vocabulary for such a little girl."

"Do I?"

"Well, yes," said Mrs. Miller, hastily changing the topic to: "Do you like the movies?"

"I really wouldn't know," said Miriam. "I've never been before."

Women began filling the lounge; the rumble of the newsreel bombs exploded in the distance. Mrs. Miller rose, tucking her purse under her arm. "I guess I'd better be running now if I want to get a seat," she said. "It was nice to have met you."

Miriam nodded ever so slightly.

It snowed all week. Wheels and footsteps moved soundlessly on the street, as if the business of living continued secretly behind a pale but impenetrable curtain. In the falling quiet there was no sky or earth, only snow lifting in the wind, frosting the window glass, chilling the rooms, deadening and hushing the city. At all hours it was necessary to keep a lamp lighted, and Mrs. Miller lost track of the days: Friday was no different from Saturday and on Sunday she went to the grocery: closed, of course.

That evening she scrambled eggs and fixed a bowl of tomato soup. Then, after putting on a flannel robe and cold-creaming her face, she propped herself up in bed with a hot-water bottle under her feet. She was reading the *Times* when the doorbell rang. At first she thought it must be a mistake and whoever it was would go away. But it rang and rang and settled to a persistent buzz. She looked at the clock: a little after eleven; it did not seem possible, she was always asleep by ten.

Climbing out of bed, she trotted barefoot across the living room. "I'm coming, please be patient." The latch was caught; she turned it this way and that way and the bell never paused an instant. "Stop it," she cried. The bolt gave way and she opened the door an inch. "What in heaven's name?"

"Hello," said Miriam.

"Oh . . . why, hello," said Mrs. Miller, stepping hesitantly into the hall. "You're that little girl."

"I thought you'd never answer, but I kept my finger on the button; I knew you were home. Aren't you glad to see me?"

Mrs. Miller did not know what to say. Miriam, she saw,

wore the same plum-velvet coat and now she had also a
beret to match; her white hair was braided in two shining
plaits and looped at the ends with enormous white ribbons.

"Since I've waited so long, you could at least let me
in," she said.

"It's awfully late. . . ."

Miriam regarded her blankly. "What difference does
that make? Let me in. It's cold out here and I have on a
silk dress." Then, with a gentle gesture, she urged Mrs.
Miller aside and passed into the apartment.

She dropped her coat and beret on a chair. She was
indeed wearing a silk dress. White silk. White silk in
February. The skirt was beautifully pleated and the
sleeves long; it made a faint rustle as she strolled about
the room. "I like your place," she said. "I like the rug,
blue's my favorite color." She touched a paper rose in a
vase on the coffee table. "Imitation," she commented
wanly. "How sad. Aren't imitations sad?" She seated
herself on the sofa, daintily spreading her skirt.

"What do you want?" asked Mrs. Miller.

"Sit down," said Miriam. "It makes me nervous to see
people stand."

Mrs. Miller sank to a hassock. "What do you want?"
she repeated.

"You know, I don't think you're glad I came."

For a second time Mrs. Miller was without an answer;

her hand motioned vaguely. Miriam giggled and pressed back on a mound of chintz pillows. Mrs. Miller observed that the girl was less pale than she remembered; her cheeks were flushed.

"How did you know where I lived?"

Miriam frowned. "That's no question at all. What's your name? What's mine?"

"But I'm not listed in the phone book."

"Oh, let's talk about something else."

Mrs. Miller said, "Your mother must be insane to let a child like you wander around at all hours of the night —and in such ridiculous clothes. She must be out of her mind."

Miriam got up and moved to a corner where a covered bird cage hung from a ceiling chain. She peeked beneath the cover. "It's a canary," she said. "Would you mind if I woke him? I'd like to hear him sing."

"Leave Tommy alone," said Mrs. Miller, anxiously. "Don't you dare wake him."

"Certainly," said Miriam. "But I don't see why I can't hear him sing." And then, "Have you anything to eat? I'm starving! Even milk and a jam sandwich would be fine."

"Look," said Mrs. Miller, rising from the hassock, "look—if I make some nice sandwiches will you be a good child and run along home? It's past midnight, I'm sure."

"It's snowing," reproached Miriam. "And cold and dark."

"Well, you shouldn't have come here to begin with," said Mrs. Miller, struggling to control her voice. "I can't help the weather. If you want anything to eat you'll have to promise to leave."

Miriam brushed a braid against her cheek. Her eyes were thoughtful, as if weighing the proposition. She turned toward the bird cage. "Very well," she said, "I promise."

How old is she? Ten? Eleven? Mrs. Miller, in the kitchen, unsealed a jar of strawberry preserves and cut four slices of bread. She poured a glass of milk and paused to light a cigarette. *And why has she come?* Her hand shook as she held the match, fascinated, till it burned her finger. The canary was singing; singing as he did in the morning and at no other time. "Miriam," she called, "Miriam, I told you not to disturb Tommy." There was no answer. She called again; all she heard was the canary. She inhaled the cigarette and discovered she had lighted the cork-tip end and—oh, really, she mustn't lose her temper.

She carried the food in on a tray and set it on the coffee table. She saw first that the bird cage still wore its night cover. And Tommy was singing. It gave her a queer sensation. And no one was in the room. Mrs. Miller went through an alcove leading to her bedroom; at the door she caught her breath.

"What are you doing?" she asked.

Miriam glanced up and in her eyes there was a look that was not ordinary. She was standing by the bureau, a jewel case opened before her. For a minute she studied Mrs. Miller, forcing their eyes to meet, and she smiled. "There's nothing good here," she said. "But I like this." Her hand held a cameo brooch. "It's charming."

"Suppose—perhaps you'd better put it back," said Mrs. Miller, feeling suddenly the need of some support. She leaned against the door frame; her head was unbearably heavy; a pressure weighted the rhythm of her heartbeat. The light seemed to flutter defectively. "Please, child—a gift from my husband . . ."

"But it's beautiful and I want it," said Miriam. *"Give it to me."*

As she stood, striving to shape a sentence which would somehow save the brooch, it came to Mrs. Miller there was no one to whom she might turn; she was alone; a fact that had not been among her thoughts for a long time. Its sheer emphasis was stunning. But here in her own room in the hushed snow-city were evidences she could not ignore or, she knew with startling clarity, resist.

Miriam ate ravenously, and when the sandwiches and milk were gone, her fingers made cobweb movements over the plate, gathering crumbs. The cameo gleamed on her blouse, the blonde profile like a trick reflection of its wearer. "That was very nice," she sighed, "though now an almond cake or a cherry would be ideal. Sweets are lovely, don't you think?"

Mrs. Miller was perched precariously on the hassock, smoking a cigarette. Her hair net had slipped lopsided and loose strands straggled down her face. Her eyes were stupidly concentrated on nothing and her cheeks were mottled in red patches, as though a fierce slap had left permanent marks.

"Is there a candy—a cake?"

Mrs. Miller tapped ash on the rug. Her head swayed slightly as she tried to focus her eyes. "You promised to leave if I made the sandwiches," she said.

"Dear me, did I?"

"It was a promise and I'm tired and I don't feel well at all."

"Mustn't fret," said Miriam. "I'm only teasing."

She picked up her coat, slung it over her arm, and arranged her beret in front of a mirror. Presently she bent close to Mrs. Miller and whispered, "Kiss me good night."

"Please—I'd rather not," said Mrs. Miller.

Miriam lifted a shoulder, arched an eyebrow. "As you like," she said, and went directly to the coffee table, seized the vase containing the paper roses, carried it to where the hard surface of the floor lay bare, and hurled it downward. Glass sprayed in all directions and she stamped her foot on the bouquet.

Then slowly she walked to the door, but before closing it she looked back at Mrs. Miller with a slyly innocent curiosity.

Mrs. Miller spent the next day in bed, rising once to feed the canary and drink a cup of tea; she took her temperature and had none, yet her dreams were feverishly agitated; their unbalanced mood lingered even as she lay staring wide-eyed at the ceiling. One dream threaded through the others like an elusively mysterious theme in a complicated symphony, and the scenes it depicted were sharply outlined, as though sketched by a hand of gifted intensity: a small girl, wearing a bridal gown and a wreath of leaves, led a gray procession down a mountain path, and among them there was unusual silence till a woman at the rear asked, "Where is she taking us?" "No one knows," said an old man marching in front. "But isn't she pretty?" volunteered a third voice. "Isn't she like a frost flower . . . so shining and white?"

Tuesday morning she woke up feeling better; harsh slats of sunlight, slanting through Venetian blinds, shed a disrupting light on her unwholesome fancies. She opened the window to discover a thawed, mild-as-spring day; a sweep of clean new clouds crumpled against a vastly blue, out-of-season sky; and across the low line of roof-tops she could see the river and smoke curving from tug-boat stacks in a warm wind. A great silver truck plowed the snow-banked street, its machine sound humming in the air.

After straightening the apartment, she went to the grocer's, cashed a check and continued to Schrafft's where she ate breakfast and chatted happily with the waitress. Oh, it was a wonderful day—more like a holiday—and it would be so foolish to go home.

She boarded a Lexington Avenue bus and rode up to Eighty-sixth Street; it was here that she had decided to do a little shopping.

She had no idea what she wanted or needed, but she idled along, intent only upon the passers-by, brisk and preoccupied, who gave her a disturbing sense of separateness.

It was while waiting at the corner of Third Avenue that she saw the man: an old man, bowlegged and stooped under an armload of bulging packages; he wore a shabby brown coat and a checkered cap. Suddenly she realized they were exchanging a smile: there was nothing friendly about this smile, it was merely two cold flickers of recognition. But she was certain she had never seen him before.

He was standing next to an El pillar, and as she crossed the street he turned and followed. He kept quite close; from the corner of her eye she watched his reflection wavering on the shopwindows.

Then in the middle of the block she stopped and faced him. He stopped also and cocked his head, grinning. But what could she say? Do? Here, in broad daylight, on Eighty-sixth Street? It was useless and, despising her own helplessness, she quickened her steps.

Now Second Avenue is a dismal street, made from scraps and ends; part cobblestone, part asphalt, part cement; and its atmosphere of desertion is permanent. Mrs. Miller walked five blocks without meeting anyone, and all the while the steady crunch of his footfalls in the snow stayed near. And when she came to a florist's shop, the sound was still with her. She hurried inside and watched through the glass door as the old man passed; he kept his eyes straight ahead and didn't slow his pace, but he did one strange, telling thing: he tipped his cap.

"Six white ones, did you say?" asked the florist. "Yes," she told him, "white roses." From there she went to a glassware store and selected a vase, presumably a replacement for the one Miriam had broken, though the price was intolerable and the vase itself (she thought) grotesquely vulgar. But a series of unaccountable purchases had begun, as if by prearranged plan: a plan of which she had not the least knowledge or control.

She bought a bag of glazed cherries, and at a place called the Knickerbocker Bakery she paid forty cents for six almond cakes.

Within the last hour the weather had turned cold again; like blurred lenses, winter clouds cast a shade over the sun, and the skeleton of an early dusk colored the sky; a damp mist mixed with the wind and the voices of a few children who romped high on mountains of gutter snow seemed lonely and cheerless. Soon the first flake fell, and when Mrs. Miller reached the brownstone house, snow was falling in a swift screen and foot tracks vanished as they were printed.

The white roses were arranged decoratively in the vase. The glazed cherries shone on a ceramic plate. The almond cakes, dusted with sugar, awaited a hand. The canary fluttered on its swing and picked at a bar of seed.

At precisely five the doorbell rang. Mrs. Miller *knew* who it was. The hem of her housecoat trailed as she crossed the floor. "Is that you?" she called.

"Naturally," said Miriam, the word resounding shrilly from the hall. "Open this door."

"Go away," said Mrs. Miller.

"Please hurry . . . I have a heavy package."

"Go away," said Mrs. Miller. She returned to the living room, lighted a cigarette, sat down and calmly listened to the buzzer; on and on and on. "You might as well leave. I have no intention of letting you in."

Shortly the bell stopped. For possibly ten minutes Mrs. Miller did not move. Then, hearing no sound, she concluded Miriam had gone. She tiptoed to the door and opened it a sliver; Miriam was half-reclining atop a cardboard box with a beautiful French doll cradled in her arms.

"Really, I thought you were never coming," she said peevishly. "Here, help me get this in, it's awfully heavy."

It was not spell-like compulsion that Mrs. Miller felt, but rather a curious passivity; she brought in the box, Miriam the doll. Miriam curled up on the sofa, not troubling to remove her coat or beret, and watched disinterestedly as Mrs. Miller dropped the box and stood trembling, trying to catch her breath.

"Thank you," she said. In the daylight she looked pinched and drawn, her hair less luminous. The French doll she was loving wore an exquisite powdered wig and its idiot glass eyes sought solace in Miriam's. "I have a surprise," she continued. "Look into my box."

Kneeling, Mrs. Miller parted the flaps and lifted out another doll; then a blue dress which she recalled as the one Miriam had worn that first night at the theater; and of the remainder she said, "It's all clothes. Why?"

"Because I've come to live with you," said Miriam, twisting a cherry stem. "Wasn't it nice of you to buy me the cherries . . . ?"

"But you can't! For God's sake go away—go away and leave me alone!"

". . . and the roses and the almond cakes? How really

wonderfully generous. You know, these cherries are delicious. The last place I lived was with an old man; he was terribly poor and we never had good things to eat. But I think I'll be happy here." She paused to snuggle her doll closer. "Now, if you'll just show me where to put my things . . ."

Mrs. Miller's face dissolved into a mask of ugly red lines; she began to cry, and it was an unnatural, tearless sort of weeping, as though, not having wept for a long time, she had forgotten how. Carefully she edged backward till she touched the door.

She fumbled through the hall and down the stairs to a landing below. She pounded frantically on the door of the first apartment she came to; a short, red-headed man answered and she pushed past him. "Say, what the hell is this?" he said. "Anything wrong, lover?" asked a young woman who appeared from the kitchen, drying her hands. And it was to her that Mrs. Miller turned.

"Listen," she cried, "I'm ashamed behaving this way but—well, I'm Mrs. H. T. Miller and I live upstairs and . . ." She pressed her hands over her face. "It sounds so absurd. . . ."

The woman guided her to a chair, while the man excitedly rattled pocket change. "Yeah?"

"I live upstairs and there's a little girl visiting me, and I suppose that I'm afraid of her. She won't leave and I can't make her and—she's going to do something terrible. She's already stolen my cameo, but she's about to do something worse—something terrible!"

The man asked, "Is she a relative, huh?"

Mrs. Miller shook her head. "I don't know who she is. Her name's Miriam, but I don't know for certain who she is."

"You gotta calm down, honey," said the woman, stroking Mrs. Miller's arm. "Harry here'll tend to this kid. Go on, lover." And Mrs. Miller said, "The door's open—5A."

After the man left, the woman brought a towel and bathed Mrs. Miller's face. "You're very kind," Mrs. Miller said. "I'm sorry to act like such a fool, only this wicked child . . ."

"Sure, honey," consoled the woman. "Now, you better take it easy."

Mrs. Miller rested her head in the crook of her arm; she was quiet enough to be asleep. The woman turned a radio dial; a piano and a husky voice filled the silence and the woman, tapping her foot, kept excellent time. "Maybe we oughta go up too," she said.

"I don't want to see her again. I don't want to be anywhere near her."

"Uh huh, but what you shoulda done, you shoulda called a cop."

Presently they heard the man on the stairs. He strode

into the room frowning and scratching the back of his neck. "Nobody there," he said, honestly embarrassed. "She musta beat it."

"Harry, you're a jerk," announced the woman. "We been sitting here the whole time and we woulda seen . . ." She stopped abruptly, for the man's glance was sharp.

"I looked all over," he said, "and there just ain't nobody there. Nobody, understand?"

"Tell me," said Mrs. Miller, rising, "tell me, did you see a large box? Or a doll?"

"No, ma'am, I didn't."

And the woman, as if delivering a verdict, said, "Well, for cryin out loud. . . ."

Mrs. Miller entered her apartment softly; she walked to the center of the room and stood quite still. No, in a sense it had not changed: the roses, the cakes, and the cherries were in place. But this was an empty room, emptier than if the furnishings and familiars were not present, lifeless and petrified as a funeral parlor. The sofa loomed before her with a new strangeness: its vacancy had a meaning that would have been less penetrating and terrible had Miriam been curled on it. She gazed fixedly at the space where she remembered setting the box and, for a moment, the hassock spun desperately. And she looked through the window; surely the river was real, surely snow was falling—but then, one could not be certain witness to anything: Miriam, so vividly *there*—and yet, where was she? Where, where?

As though moving in a dream, she sank to a chair. The room was losing shape; it was dark and getting darker and there was nothing to be done about it; she could not lift her hand to light a lamp.

Suddenly, closing her eyes, she felt an upward surge, like a diver emerging from some deeper, greener depth. In times of terror or immense distress, there are moments when the mind waits, as though for a revelation, while a skein of calm is woven over thought; it is like a sleep, or a supernatural trance; and during this lull one is aware of a force of quiet reasoning: well, what if she had never really known a girl named Miriam? that she had been foolishly frightened on the street? In the end, like everything else, it was of no importance. For the only thing she had lost to Miriam was her identity, but now she knew she had found again the person who lived in this room, who cooked her own meals, who owned a canary, who was someone she could trust and believe in: Mrs. H. T. Miller.

Listening in contentment, she became aware of a double sound: a bureau drawer opening and closing; she seemed to hear it long after completion—opening and closing. Then gradually, the harshness of it was replaced by the murmur of a silk dress and this, delicately faint, was moving nearer and swelling in intensity till the walls trembled with the vibration and the room was caving under a wave of whispers. Mrs. Miller stiffened and opened her eyes to a dull, direct stare.

"Hello," said Miriam.

THE HOME FRONT

Jean Stafford

IN THE BACK yard of the lodging house, in the top of a dead tree, glib blackbirds swung in the wind on their individual twigs. Now and again, at some signal, they dropped to the ground but presently returned in a flutter of wings. Then the fancy would strike them to clear the tree, every man jack of them and off they would go like a whole company of hysterical busybodies. All the while they were fussing, big silver gulls sailed at their ease, high above them, descending occasionally to sit on the edge of a moored fishing boat that slowly turned round and round at the head of the little harbor. Some of the gulls set out to sea, as straight and sure in their flight as though a great hand carried them out beyond the causeway to the Sound. A savage sunset ignited the windows of defense plants across the water, caused derelict heaps of rubbish to glitter blindingly, smote the khaki wings of helicopters which all day long gyrated over the disheveled land.

Although it was late in April and the day had been warm, the room was chilly and the stout doctor, shivering, drew the heavy Paisley shawl closer about his shoulders, sighed, and settled more firmly into the rocking chair by the window. Steadfastly he stared out. It would be self-indulgent to turn away in displeasure from all the symbols he read in his prospect, unprofitable to admit the intrusion of homesickness or vexation. (He had, of necessity, come to this twilight discipline; in days past he had been so imprudent in his revery that he had often lost all perspective and had thought of the war as a deliberate insult to himself.) And, indeed, it was not so much sad or vexing as it was puzzling that he, a homeless man, native of a distant country, was willy-nilly a part of the "home front," sharing richly in the spoils. As he followed the ascent of a helicopter, he marveled as frequently he did at the wonderful aptness of the phrase, "the home front." Here people lived as headily and impermanently as soldiers on battlefields. There seemed to be no natives unless the babies born here during this long pause could be called such. No indigenous architecture was visible. Probably it existed but it was hidden away behind blocks of temporary structures, by barrack-like apartment houses, sprawling into the yards of churches, huddling in the sulphurous shadows of factories. And although everything was new, made freshly for this especial period in the world's history, it had a second-hand look. Houses, oil drums, buses, people seemed to have been got at a fire sale.

There was a perpetual stirring in the lodging house. All the other tenants were defense workers, and the walls of the corridors were hung with warning pennants: "QUIET! BULLARD WORKER! HELP HIM HELP WIN THE WAR!" At the most unseemly hours—eleven at night, four in the morning—alarm clocks shrieked, taps gushed, feet crunched over the gravel of the driveway to the never ending stream of buses. The lodgers ranged from late adolescence to early senility and they came from all over the country, from Harrisburg, Pennsylvania; Pueblo, Colorado; Mobile; Galveston; Wilmington, Delaware. They lived three to a room and six to a bathroom and because there were so many of them and their existence was so migratory, it was impossible to tell them apart, to give them more specific designations than "old" and "young," "male" and "female." Dr. Pakheiser from time to time received bits of information about them from the Hungarian manageress, Mrs. Horvath. She tossed them to him, dry and meatless, and did so without the least good humor. On the first floor there was (or had been) a Sikorsky worker who owned a fishing boat and on Sundays went to the Sound for bass. A lady accountant at Remington Arms had left her electric grill on for six hours and the pan that had been on it melted down to nothing, creating a fearful stink. A foreman at the Bunner Ritter plant had been rejected by the Army for ulcers of the stomach. A girl at Chance Vought had, returning from a weekend in Massachusetts, seen a trainload of prisoners of war passing through the station in Providence and she had reported that they grinned shamelessly as if they were on a holiday. But the doctor did not know whether these adventures belonged to current tenants or to former ones, and if he had inquired further and had correctly assigned the histories to the right names and faces, it would have served no purpose; by the time he was sure of his ground, they would have packed up their suitcases and moved away and immediately been replaced.

He was sympathetic with their restlessness but sternly held himself detached from it. Had he not done so, he, too, probably would have wandered from one boarding house to the next like a sick person constantly shifting about in his bed trying to find a comfortable position for his aching bones. Refusing to think of himself as a "transient," pretending that there would never be an end to the war or to this exile, he had put up with the chilliness of the house, the unpleasant manner of the manageress, the excessive rent, and had furthermore doggedly trans-

formed the room into *his* room as if he were going to live
in it the rest of his life. It was the first time in his three
years of residence in America that he had accomplished
the transformation, and it had not been easy. In former
rooms, though, it had been impossible. This was like one
in a hotel which defied any eccentric impress, and in the
beginning he had almost despaired, had been convinced
that like all the others, it would remain inviolably and
complacently itself and that when he finally went away,
if his signature were there at all, it would be nothing
more characteristic of him than of the tenants before him
or the ones to follow: a half-used box of toothpowder and
a rusted razor blade in the medicine chest, or on the desk
a bottle of ink or a glass ashtray bought for a dime. There
was, upon everything, the mark of an absolute and
wholly impersonal vulgarity. The furniture was mongrel.
The walls were cream-colored plaster that could offend
no one; fastened to them here and there were besilvered
lamps containing bulbs shaped like fat candleflames that
shed a pale and genteel light. The rugs were scrupulously
unobtrusive. The sturdy column of the standing lamp was
embellished with twists of iron that represented nothing
on earth, and the shade, seemingly designed to diminish
illumination by exactly half, was silk of a color that could
not be named, a color like one acquired by an amateur
chemist or by a child experimenting with crayons. The
ample bed (too ample for his understanding. It was called

a "three-quarter" bed and he wondered whether it was meant for two children or for someone prodigiously obese) was covered with a faded counterpane made of two Indian prints sewn together.

But the room had its virtues. The rocking chair was comfortable, the table was steady, and there were plenty of clothes hangers in the closet. And Mrs. Horvath kept everything clean. Aside from the fireplace which he had been requested not to use, and the only mirror which was hopelessly defective, and the writing desk which had a limping leg, everything was in "good working order."

The exterior of the house was equally noncommittal. It was large, shapeless and built of yellow stone. It stood behind a high brick wall, its back windows overlooking an arm of the sea which, at low tide, was a black and stinking mudflat. A dump had been made at the end of the water and here was heaped all the frightful refuse of the city, the high-heeled shoes and the rotten carrots and the abused insides of automobiles; when the wind blew, the odor from the dump was so putrid in so individual a way that it was quite impossible to describe. But on a clear day, the doctor could look the other way and see, far off, the live blue Sound and the silhouettes of white sailboats and gray battleships. And while the plants, their windows ghastly blue all night, their noises constant every hour of every day, were almost within a stone's throw of his window, he had at least the illusion of being in the country. For the lawns in front and in back were healthy, the trees were abundant, and forsythia was blooming now along the wall. He had pondered often in the year he had lived here why so expensive a house (for clearly it was that; its plate glass and the intricate furbelows of its façade testified to suddenly acquired money) had been built on so unprepossessing a site, and at last he learned from a taxi-driver that the original owner had been a rumrunner who had brought his boats up the narrow neck of water and had unloaded them at the cottage in the back yard where now the Horvath family lived. While he was unable to find more than a humorous token in it, he thought with certain pleasure of the interview in which the house had changed hands and become the property of the present landlord, a Roman Catholic priest.

Sometimes, too, he wondered how the bootlegger would regard the changes he had made in his room, a room which perhaps had formerly been the office for the transaction of his illegal business. And how, for that matter, the priest did when he came on his monthly tour of inspection. Very likely both of them would find it prissy and impractical. He had taken down the pictures he found there: a tinted photograph of the Grand Canyon (which he thought must be the most dreadful sight in the world), a subdued study of an English cottage and one of a vase of asters. In their place he had hung a print of

"The Siege of Toledo" and one of "The Fall of Icarus" and a photograph of the bridge in Würzburg. On top of the bookcase were three decanters, for kümmel, brandy and Dubonnet, a little white pot of philodendron, and a pewter tray on which stood two heavy wine glasses and a curious pipe. In the shelves were the few books he had brought with him from Ludwigshafen: Dante, Rilke, Plato, some medical books, *Buddenbrooks*, *Crime and Punishment*, *The Charterhouse of Parma*, and those he had bought here, in the hope, never realized, of learning to read English easily. Those were *For Whom the Bell Tolls*, *The Late George Apley*, *The Golden Treasury* and *The Story of San Michele*. A cuckoo clock hung on the wall over the bed and on the bureau a large wooden nutcracker lay amongst big pecans in a polished lemonwood bowl. On the bedside table were an ashtray he had bought in Milan, a brown earthenware carafe, a diary bound in green leather, and a silver letter opener.

When, at nightfall, he drew the windowblinds against industrial America, it was not hard to imagine himself in his student room at Heidelberg. He had never been rich enough to eat at the town restaurants and he had disliked the tepid white food at the Mensa of the University, and so he had made little suppers for himself at his desk. And while now he was quite able to afford four-course dinners (the dearth of doctors for civilians had contrived for him a flourishing and gainful practice amongst Hungarian defense workers and their pregnant wives) he preferred to remain in his room and eat the sort of food he had done when he was a young man. Upon the table he would place the parcels he had brought from the delicatessen: a little sausage and a loaf of bread, a bottle of pickled tomatoes, a carton of Schmierkäse, perhaps a jar of marinated herring. Then, his meal ready, he would pour himself a glass of Dubonnet, light an Egyptian Prettiest cigarette and sit for a while in the chair by the window, staring now at the dark green blind that was punctured here and there, admitting star-like bits of light.

During the day, Dr. Pakheiser smoked American cigarettes, but he had found that nothing so completely and happily restored his student days to him as the smell of Oriental tobacco, and because he was so busy until he left his office, he could not afford time for the nostalgic meditations it brought. Closing his eyes, he would fancy himself twenty years younger, not yet fat, but even now near-sighted, eating ham and bread and drinking *Rotwein* in the narrow room of Frau Jost's flat. Frau Jost was a pretty, friendly young widow about whom he sometimes had romantic daydreams, and she had a daughter of four, a jolly little girl named Greta. Every morning, as Alfred left the house, Greta came to wish him good-by. She clutched in her arms a black cat who wore a red ribbon about its neck. And as he ran down the stairs, she always said, "Please look up at the window, Herr Pakheiser, and I will wave." Outside, in the steep street, he had to hold his head far back so that he could see the top window, and there she was, on time and faithful every day, to wave her hand and smile at him, still holding her cat.

Although those years at Heidelberg had been rich and full of importance, it was little Greta Jost that the flavor of the cigarette brought back most clearly. While he had had friends with whom he played chess at Burkhardt's *Konditorei* and had drunk with on Saturday nights at the Vater Rhein and while he had even occasionally had a girl, it was his daily encounter with the child that seemed now to fix the days of the past. He had been, even then, a person of strict habit. Once Greta had had chicken-pox and for a week had not appeared at the window, and all that time Alfred had been somewhat inattentive to his lectures and had spent more time at Burkhardt's. But strangely enough, he had not really been fond of Greta —children, in general, made him shy—and he had even found himself wishing that the ritual had never been established since once it had been it had to be repeated every day without fail for his complete peace of mind. He was even annoyed if the cat did not appear at the window or if it appeared without its ribbon.

But what he would not give for Greta now! With a perversity which he acknowledged frankly, he imagined that he had been devoted to her, that he had called her

pet names and had dandled her on his knee. And that his
relationship with her mother had been intimate. He
could even long for the irascible porter at the medical
college, for the torpid *Badmeister* at the public baths who
invariably tried to give him a towel which someone else
had just finished using. All these people whom he had
known slightly or not at all seemed, in his misshapen
reflection, to be his friends.

Dr. Pakheiser was not given to self-pity. A scientific
man, he looked on facts. He knew that the *Badmeister* had
no more been his friend than was Mrs. Horvath and that,
in the end, Greta was the only one who had that stature.
And just so now, twenty years later, he had again one
friend, one companion, a solitary daily relation with a
breathing creature. His companion was a gray tom-cat
who called on him each evening with the same unswerv-
ing regularity that had brought the little girl to the window every morning. The cat came at seven o'clock, an-
nouncing himself with a trilling mew outside the door.
He drank the heavy cream his host had poured into a
bowl for him and then he spent the evening, until about
midnight, curled up in the doctor's lap, asleep. Two or
three times in the course of the evening, he roused himself to make an excursion round the room, cleverly picking his way through the decanters, patting the trailing
leaves of the philodendron to watch them sway. He
washed a little and returned and slept again. Half-roused

by the turning of a page or the sound of a match being struck, he would briefly purr as if to say that his affection had not lessened, that he was merely preoccupied. At midnight, Dr. Pakheiser took him downstairs, dropped him on the veranda and watched him, revived by the night air, streak across the lawn and disappear over the wall.

The doctor called him Milenka which in Russian, of which he knew a few words, means "darling." He knew too little Russian, even, to affix the masculine diminutive. "Milenka," he would say, "I-yi-yi-yi, bad puss! Bad boy. Ah, Milenka!" Milenka was an ordinary gray cat with white mittens, a white snout and a shell-pink nose. He was rather ugly, for he was underdeveloped and rangy and since he spent a good part of the day in the coal bin, his paws were always smudged. But he had a full, healthy purr and a gentle nature. Rarely did he strop his claws on the carpet, and thanks to the doctor's weekly application of One Spot powder, he had very few fleas.

Dr. Pakheiser realized once with half-ashamed amusement that he had for Milenka a real love, whereas for Greta he had had only a perfunctory gratitude. It was chiefly, he supposed, because he was the cat's protector as well as his friend and had it not been for his suppers of cream and herring, the poor thing would have had to shift for himself on the dump. Indeed, he was quite sure that if he moved away, Mrs. Horvath would have the cat destroyed, for she had not known, she declared cantankerously, when she took over the job, that she would have an animal to care for as well as beds and bathtubs. No one knew where Milenka had come from. The landlord disclaimed all knowledge of him; the former manageress denied that she had ever fed him or invited him in any way to stay.

The doctor neither liked nor disliked animals. He had always been indifferent to them, save for police dogs whom he feared and cocker spaniels whom he scorned for their somehow homosexual softness. He had never known an individual dog or cat well. So this strong feeling about Milenka perplexed him. Was he turning into an old lady? And would he, together with his cat-fancying, get notions before he was fifty? But these speculations did not really worry him; he was sure that his fundamental motive in helping the cat survive was that he did not like Mrs. Horvath and by his lavish purchases of fish and cream, he was deviously repaying her for her impertinences.

Mrs. Horvath was a dirty, dumpy person in a brown coverall and a blue work shirt. She was anti-Semitic in the most extraordinarily forthright way Dr. Pakheiser had ever seen. On the first day of her regime she had been introduced to the doctor by the departing manageress, and she had said, "I think you are Jew, Doctor. But I get rent every Wednesday all same. You don't worry." Each time he recollected this speech (delivered with a smile which could not have disarmed a child) he was so taken aback that he was never able to analyze exactly what she meant. Evidently it was her intention to announce her antipathy to Jews at the very outset so that her tenant would not start off under a misapprehension. It became clear, after a few days, that her rule was firm: she decidedly was not one of those people who say, "Some of my best friends are Jews." On the contrary, she would say, "I hate all Jews." In a way, he preferred her attitude to that, say, of his office girl, Miss Johnson, who, with aggressive piety, often congratulated him on being one of the chosen people. With Mrs. Horvath, he was dealing with an armed enemy and war, with her, was war. Miss Johnson, on the other hand, while less wounding, was more treacherous. She could catch him offguard when he was fatigued and, sympathizing with him for being uprooted from his country, could make him prey to a burning, unobjectified anger on behalf of his whole race, and to a weepy grief for himself. Then he would despise America, Connecticut, his cramped and cluttered office, the strapping great charwoman who cleaned it, the smell of workmen in the waiting room and of workmen's cigarettes, but most of all he would despise Miss Johnson.

Milenka was the immediate cause of war between Mrs. Horvath and Dr. Pakheiser. About two weeks after her arrival, she came one evening to collect the rent. Seeing the cat curled up on the pillow of the bed, she wrinkled her low forehead, bunched up her flat Magyar nose and said, "Cat! I *like* dog. I *like* cat. But outside. Not in the house. In Europe, we have dog, we have cat, but all outside. Inside they make their doing on the carpet and all where. Outside, Doctor, I must ask you." Dr. Pakheiser, unnerved, a man who preferred on all occasions to agree, cried, "I see!" and pretended to himself that this was only a humorous crotchet she was airing conversationally. But she remained firm in the doorway even after he had given her the money and then, so suddenly that he scarcely realized what was happening, she bounded forward toward the bed, shrieking, "Out! Out, you!" and Milenka, his eyes widening with terror, leaped from the bed and ran out the door.

The next evening, though, admitted to the house by the man who left for the graveyard shift at Chance Vought, the cat came back, and the doctor, emboldened by his desire for company and his need for continuing custom, again opened his door. Every night thereafter, except on Wednesday when the rent was due, he came and was not turned away. Mrs. Horvath, to be sure, was aware of what was going on. In the morning when the doctor went downstairs, he usually found her indolently flicking a dust cloth over the newel post or frankly reading the lodgers' postal cards or sitting, sprawled like a big tom-boy, in one of the chairs of the foyer. She would give

him a look half scornful, half angry and would say, "I
don't know what happen to you when Father come and
see those places on the carpet with sausage marks." Or
she would tell him, jeeringly, that Father was going to be
outraged when he saw the hole in the curtain the cat had
clawed. "I tell *you,* Doctor," she would say, "on the
grass, okay when they lose their hair. Outside, all right.
Inside, on the cushions, hell's bells!" Sometimes she
would simply ask him, in the derisive voice of a bad
schoolboy, "How you find Milenka last night, Doctor?
Plenty good fleas on him, eh?" And once, reaching the
limit of her insolence, she followed him out the door and
paced up the driveway, calling shrilly, "Milenka!
Milenka!"

When he was not in school, the manageress was accom-
panied by her thirteen-year-old son, a large boy with a
malicious face that forever grinned under a sailor cap.
Occasionally it was he who came for the rent and Dr.
Pakheiser, fumbling in his wallet, felt that the boy with
his obscene leer had expected to find dirty French pictures on the wall or a light woman in the bed. "Hey,
Doc," he said once, "you like that cat?" And the doctor,
laughing violently, replied, "Ach, yes! Very much."
Freddie continued. Pretty soon now "that cat" had better
watch its step for he was going to trap and tame some
birds and if that dope of an old gray dumbbell got one
of them, it would be "good-by, cat." Dr. Pakheiser,

baffled by the assurance of the outsized youth, cried, "Ach, so!" louder and more amiably than ever.

So far, no birds had been caught, but Freddie, on Saturday and Sunday, worked all day long making his traps out of wooden crates, and in time the back yard was so full of them that it appeared he intended to catch entire flocks. And the doctor had no doubt either that Milenka would chase the birds or that Freddie would cruelly punish him.

II

On this damp April evening, Dr. Pakheiser was about to draw his windowblinds and prepare his supper when he saw Mr. Horvath come out of the cottage bringing a step-ladder which he set up underneath an apple tree. At his approach, the blackbirds all flew off, twittering irritably. Some time before, he had built a bonfire at the water's edge which now was burning brightly, sending up bits of charred paper, like smaller blackbirds. The man called out, "Hey, Freddie, come here a minute." And Freddie came charging through the door, wearing a baseball mitt on one hand. There was a colloquy which the doctor could not hear and then the boy, rushing to the bonfire, hurling his mitt to the ground, cried, "Oh, boy!" He lighted a torch and came back to the step-ladder, sedately so that the flame would not go out, handed it to his father and then climbed up. At the top, he wavered a little and let out an exclamation of fright, but he regained his balance and stooped down to receive the torch. He was just tall enough to reach the puffy white tent of caterpillars in a high crotch of the tree. The doctor watched, sickened, saw yellow flames shoot up as the fat tumor caught fire. Freddie had not thought ahead. A worm fell upon his upturned face and he screamed with revulsion and let the torch drop to the ground where it went on burning and sending up black smoke. The work, though, was done and while his father beat the caterpillars to death with the back of a shovel where they had fallen in the grass, the boy came down the ladder and went toward the cottage, wiping his face with both hands as though it never would be clean again. Mr. Horvath laughed at him and went on killing the pests. Mrs. Horvath came to the screen door and hooted at her son, "Ha! Ha!" she laughed. "You keep the mouth open next time and see what comes in." Restored to his normal spirits, Freddie hooted back, "Yeah, like fun I will! Yeah, in a pig's valise I will!"

There was a miaow at the doctor's door. He drew down the windowblind sharply, shuddering at what he had just seen. There was something primeval in those people; their communal enjoyment of the annihilation of the caterpillars was so stupid and so brutish that the doctor actually retched. Then he let in the refined, soft-moving cat.

"I-yi-yi-yi!" he said, stooping to pick Milenka up. "I-yi-yi-yi, my bad puss, my bad boy." Milenka stretched his head forward and rubbed the top of it against Dr. Pakheiser's chin, purring loudly. "Milenka," murmured the man. "Ah, my good friend; my dearest one." He poured the cream into the cereal bowl, fetched a quart of Irish ale from the widow sill and, sitting down, said to his companion, *"Gut Mahlzeit."*

When they had both finished and the doctor had put away the food, he settled once more in the rocking chair with the brandy decanter at his elbow. He opened the journal that had come that day and began methodically with the first article, one on the use of sulfa drugs in the treatment of sinusitis. He had read only a few sentences when Milenka leaped to his lap. Dr. Pakheiser ran his fingers under the cat's jaw and around the ears, laid his whole hand on the little gray belly to feel the vibration and read on, at last in repose now that his house was complete. But there was an uneasiness stirring at the back of his mind and although he concentrated and extracted the full meaning from all he read that night, he observed when he rose at twelve to put Milenka out that he had drunk three times as much brandy as was his custom and had made a great inroad into the package of Egyptian Prettiests which he never smoked after supper.

That night he had a strange dream. He dreamed of D-day. He and little Greta Jost had come to wish Mr. Horvath good luck and they had set out to find rooms.

The hotels were crowded, for the holiday throngs were tremendous. They sauntered up the boardwalk, admiring the bright tailored shingle where fashionable people were gathered for the start of the regatta. They entered a hotel which was quite deserted save for a man sitting alone on a little mezzanine at one end of the lobby. He sat at a round amethyst-colored glass table, drinking a very pink cocktail, and as they approached, he stood up smiling and cordially extending his hand. They recognized the President and they were gratified when he called them both by name. His address was old-fashioned: he said "Miss Greta" and "Mr. Alfred." Linking arms, the three of them went out. The President said that while he wished the invasion to be as leisurely as possible, it would be folly, would it not, to give the signal too late in the day? Did not his young friends agree that despite our great advances in electricity, there was something essentially *better* about sunlight? Never was there so civilized a man! In the pure, brilliant sky, exquisite airplanes circled and swooped like the loveliest of birds. There was such a profusion of scarlet! In the flags, in the hats of the spectators, on the wings of planes, in colossal bouquets in vases a mile high situated on the beach at intervals of fifteen yards. The yachts were all ready, freshly painted, brightly bannered for the race to Europe.

Alfred and Greta were the first to land. As they walked up the ramp, he noticed the tiny Scotch plaid ribbons that bound her pigtails. Wandering, they could not find the *Konditorei* he had suggested although time and time again they set forth from the Heiliggeist cathedral and took the familiar street. Nor was it possible, as formerly, to see the ruined castle from the bridge, and Greta said, "Herr Pakheiser, I don't believe this is Heidelberg. Now I am afraid and I want my mother. I think we have come to Heilbronn by mistake." But Alfred pointed to the marking that clearly read, "Philosophen Weg," and he soothed her, "Don't be frightened, dearest." They were speeding in a dirty express train through Freiburg, its towers and steeples flattened out like any corpse, its vineyards wasted with drought and disease. The Alps diminished as they neared them. No trees were left. The sun was small and red like an ember. Alfred, receiving a wicker-covered jug of wine from a weeping man who shared their compartment, was too touched and too embarrassed to begin a conversation, but at last he thought of something. "Sir," he said solemnly, "sir, did you ever go fishing in the Sound for bass, using a caddis worm as bait?" The wine in the man's throat gurgled like a death rattle as he looked out at the leveled mountains. "There was a short notice in some review or other," he said, "outlined in black. Even so . . . even so . . ."

In the limbo where he waited a moment before he wakened fully, he thought he was writing the opening paragraph of a children's story in which a little boy lay on his stomach drinking water from a stream. Suddenly his eyes encountered two others, hooded, sparkling with some horrible intelligence. They belonged to a monstrous caddis worm which advanced through the water as he withdrew.

He woke violently. He clasped his hands to his forehead and in the darkness softly moaned. "I must control myself. I must not perish here."

III

Late in May, Milenka disappeared. Dr. Pakheiser was disturbed but not really anxious until the fourth night passed and he still dined alone. On the fifth morning he diffidently asked Mrs. Horvath if she had seen the cat, and he detected something doubtful, something covert in her reply. She was not arrogant and her eyes seemed unable to focus on his face. She said—uncomfortably, it seemed to him—"No, Doctor. I see him Sunday. My husband see him Sunday. He come back, don't you worry." Then she looked directly at him and smiled, "He know where his sardine is, I tell you." The doctor was smoking and as he went to the table to drop a long ash into the tray there, his hand abruptly shook and the ashes fell to the carpet. He and the woman both briefly looked at them, dispersed fanwise on the green border. And he knew then that she was hiding something, for she did not reproach him for his clumsiness even though she had just finished using the carpet sweeper. He was so angry that he stumbled to the door and his rage so blinded him that he had to lean against the jamb a moment before he could see the steps. It was not, at this moment, that he was mourning the loss of Milenka; it was that he had sensed, despite her near-civility and his own timorousness, as killing a hatred between them as though they were two jungle beasts, determined to destroy one another. "If she has killed my cat," he brooded as he drove through the gate, "then I . . ." but he could not finish the sentence. He could devise no penalty high enough for such wickedness, no penance sufficiently humiliating.

For two weeks nothing passed between the manageress and her lodger. Nothing, that is, but glances boldly indignant on the doctor's part, guilty on the woman's. It seemed to him that the life of the rest of the house had ceased, that all was at an ominous standstill before a final battle to the death. And then, incredibly, the cat came back. When he first heard the mewing outside his door on the dot of seven, Dr. Pakheiser could not believe his ears. Not until the sound had been repeated two or three times did he open the door. His joy at the reunion was less than his shame for falsely accusing Mrs. Horvath and less than his bewilderment at her shifty-eyed embarrassment. Apparently Milenka had just wandered off somewhere as tom-cats do in the spring. He was thin and mangy and his coat was matted with cockleburs and beggar's-lice. His purr had a bronchial rasp and the doctor made a note on his memorandum pad to bring home a worm pill the next night. Nor had he any appetite for the bit of herring which was all that the doctor had to offer him, and after less than half an hour, he asked to be let out. But this strangeness, under good care, would pass. That night the doctor slept well.

"Good morning," he cried heartily as he met Mrs. Horvath in the hall the following day. "Have you seen my friend, Mrs. Horvath? He came back for his sardine as you promised me."

The woman's eyes opened from their sleepiness, her lips parted in disbelief, and she said, "Back? That cat back?" Dr. Pakheiser assured her that what he said was true and at the moment, to confirm him, Milenka leaped to the window sill from the veranda and sat there in profile, blinking his eyes. Mrs. Horvath stared, "I do not know," she said. "It is like a dream." The doctor surmised, then, that the cat had been put into a bag and taken into the country somewhere and been abandoned. It was scarcely believable that he could be so gross as to laugh triumphantly and almost to sob his words: "Yes, Mrs. Horvath, my dearest friend is restored to me!"

She looked away from the window. "But, Doctor, I do not know. My son, he catch birds all while now. His school finish pretty soon. I think he don't want that cat here."

"It is cruel to catch birds," he said severely, no longer tyrannized over by her now that he had got his cat back. "And *I* want him here even if that boy doesn't." It gave him pleasure to say "that boy" just as she and her son spoke of "that cat."

"But, Doctor, the cat kill birds. My boy don't kill them. He make them into good pet."

"It is the cat's nature to kill birds. But it is not the nature of man to take prisoners."

"No?" she said. The look of cunning returned to her face. "What we fight war for, then, Doctor?"

"I don't know, Mrs. Horvath, I am sure." He was overpowered with disgust that he should be haggling with this obtuse woman over the life of a diseased cat, and that he should be confronted by so irrelevant a question which he could not answer and which, in spite of its fatuous context, made him feel that because he could only say he did not know, like an unprepared schoolboy, his mind was growing dull. And just as he was preparing to bid the manageress good morning and to hurry to his office to plunge himself into work, she threw out a remark more imbecilic than the first but one that utterly confounded him. She said, "My son protect birds from cats just like America protect Jews from Hitler."

For a moment, before he had collected himself, he

read an awful symbolic wisdom into this absurdity. Un-
hampered by learning, in a country where she could not
read the language and could barely speak it, where she
could be influenced only by the most basic of national
prejudices and loyalties, she was truly a natural enemy.
Here was the perfect, the pure hatred; the real thing was
in Mrs. Horvath's simple heart. He was not so far gone
yet as to think that she was bent on getting rid of the cat
out of vengeance. Her reasons were more human than
that; she did not like cats and she wanted to indulge her
son. But at the same time, there was something so sure
in her figure of speech that it was as if, from now on, she
would implicitly believe it, would even repeat it in later
conversations.

In reply, Dr. Pakheiser only smiled. On his way out,
he gave Milenka a pat on the head and said loudly, "I-yi-
yi-yi, bad puss!" and walked jauntily round the house to
his car, whistling. Whistling, as the phrase went, in the
dark.

All spring, Dr. Pakheiser trod on eggs. Each evening
when he came home and parked his car in the back yard
where Freddie was at work on his bird traps, his heart
constricted with apprehension. This would be the night,
he thought, when Milenka would not come. The boy,
grinning even as he pounded in the nails, looked up with
a dispassionate greeting. "Hi, Doc. This is for me to get
an oriole in, see? And that there one is for me to get me

a purple grackle in. I lure 'em—I know how they whistle and I whistle and they think I'm a bird—and then they get in this little place here, see, and I pull a string and the door comes down and they can't get out. And then I get 'em so tame they'll eat right out of my hand." Once or twice the doctor inquired about his school with the intention of keeping things running smoothly between them. He went to the nuns to whom he referred collectively as "Sister." "Sister flunked me in Latin but she gave me B in Algebra and D plus in English." But it bored him to talk about the contents of his days; he would break off suddenly and pointing to the blackbirds in the dead tree would say, "See them? I don't want 'em but I could have 'em all if I did." And the doctor would look up at the crowded branches, object of his dreamy contemplation every day. "They're dumb birds," Freddie would say as he threw a pebble into the tree and they all disbanded. "They don't know where they're at." Dr. Pakheiser would reply, "I don't think any birds at all know where they're at." They had come to this conventional rite through a mutual understanding: the doctor disliked birds, the boy disliked cats. Neither spoke of his aversion, but under their banter was the serious warning, "Your pet stays where it belongs, or else."

Milenka was soon prospering. His coat came in soft and shining; his purr cleared and his eyes lost the milkiness that had clouded them when he first came home. He was full grown now and, obliged to assume the responsibilities of a male animal, sometimes missed a meal and spent the time with a plump old tabby who howled for him on the stone wall. But good friend that Milenka was, if he failed to come one evening, he sneaked through the door early the next morning when someone went out to the day-shift. The doctor came to enjoy these morning visits even more than the evening ones. He would go back to bed after he had poured out the cream and lie there watching; when the cat had finished, he would jump to the bed, walk carefully up Dr. Pakheiser's legs to the thigh and there establish himself. But there was one drawback to his coming in the daytime. Ironically, a pair of wrens had built a nest under the eave of the corner window and Milenka, hearing them rustle and chirp, would sit up, his whiskers twitching, his sleek little body poised for a leap. And whenever this happened, Dr. Pakheiser felt a thrill of disquiet, afraid the cat would commit a crime during the day while he was at his office and could not intercede for him.

Just as Milenka thrived, so did Freddie's successes multiply and by the first of June, the clumsy home-made cages in the garage were half full of orioles and robins and finches and flickers which, at feeding time, gave out a dissonant and reedy clamor. One Sunday afternoon, when school was over for him and the skies were full of birds, Freddie stalked a robin in full view of the doctor's windows. He crept across the lawn on his hands and knees toward the large unmoving bird. The advance could either have been for the purpose of murder or for ministration to an injured wing. It was beautiful to watch. There was no sudden nervous jerking, no change of pace. When he was within two feet of the bird, his hands left the ground and his lips parted in his earnestness. His posture and his skill made the doctor think of a praying mantis, one of those miraculously ugly creatures which he had seen on the road under a tulip tree and had taken at first for withering seed pods. Now, a foot away, the hands parted. He was ready for the capture. Dr. Pakheiser found himself holding his breath and could not tell whether he wanted the bird to foil the boy or wished to see it taken. Directly under the certain hands, the prey was still unaware. Now they descended and gently took the bird. Freddie stroked its head tenderly with his forefinger and when the captive made a movement to escape, he drew it to his chest smiling rapturously. And the doctor might have warmed toward him, seeing the innocent happiness in his face, had he not bawled out, "Hey, Mom! Got me another one. Boy, oh, boy, am I *good!*"

IV

Its head high, its tail feathers trailing the ground, the great cock-pheasant moved with dignity out of the

shadow of the apple tree into the light where all the glory
of its habiliments shone like a sun-struck diamond. Dr.
Pakheiser, who had been roused early by an urgent telephone call, paused in his dressing to watch the wonderful
bird. He had never seen one before save in pictures
which he had not altogether believed. The japanning of
its plumage had been masterful: emerald blazed forth
beside gold and gold beside scarlet. There was something about it so rich and unusual that he did not think
of it as a bird at all but as a costly ornament for the patch
of bright grass where now it stopped, surveying the ter-
rain as if this were its own dominion. But the kingly
creature was no wiser than its plebeian brothers, and it
began to walk rapidly toward one of Freddie's traps. The
doctor immediately flung wide his window, unfastened
the screen and leaned out, shouting and waving his arms
to scare away the foolish bird. He disturbed the sleeping
wrens in the eave and they flew wildly against the screen,
then sailed off to the apple tree. But the pheasant was
deaf to warnings and walked complacently toward his
prison. In a frenzy, Dr. Pakheiser reached back to the
bedside table and picked up his metal ashtray from
Milan. He hurled it at the pheasant. It fell close to the
quick feet and instantly the bird turned, running, this
time, back over the grass through the shadow of the
apple tree and disappeared in the tall weeds that grew
about the abandoned boats. Freddie ran out of the cot-

tage. The doctor fastened his screen and stepped back out of sight behind the drapery at the window, but he watched the boy whose face was contorted with fury and frustration. Tears began as he picked up the ashtray. For a second he stared at it as if he were not sure what to do with it and then, with a bawl, he flung it into the water which was at low tide and, cursing at the top of his voice, went indoors.

Dr. Pakheiser finished dressing. He knew that he was not steady enough to shave, but he washed his face and hands slowly and thoroughly, using the nail brush with unaccustomed vigor. He lighted a cigarette and sat down, aware that his delay was selfish. But his patient seemed remote, the illness unimportant. It was not until the cigarette had burned down to nothing that he got up, found his hat and went out. He stole quietly down the stairs and round the house. There was no sign of life in the back yard. From within the cottage came the sound of Mrs. Horvath's voice; she spoke loudly but in Hungarian and he understood nothing of what she said. He gained his car and he was safe. But he knew that the score was not yet settled, for as he drove away, he saw Freddie's face at the window, the strange Mongolian nose spread out as it pressed against the pane. This, finally, would be the day of reckoning.

When he came home at five that afternoon, Dr. Pakheiser found both Mrs. Horvath and Freddie in the large front bedroom downstairs. Someone had just moved out and they were making it ready for a new tenant. They were turning the mattress, but when they saw the doctor, they stopped, the great thing folded halfway over and held in their strong red hands.

Mrs. Horvath said, "Good night, Doctor. I bring you ashtray tomorrow. You lose your blue one?" He had not anticipated so devious an attack and he was nonplused. Since all three of them knew well enough that the ashtray was lying in the mud, it was absurd to carry on her game, to say, for example, that he had taken it to the office. And so he replied ambiguously, "Oh, thank you. If you have an extra one, I will be glad to have it." He started toward the stairs, but they had not finished with him yet.

Mrs. Horvath said, "Was it a good day, Doctor?"

"A busy day," he said, "But, yes, a good one, I think."

The boy, his chin upon the mound of the mattress, fixed him with the fearless eye of the insulted child and slowly said, "It wasn't a good day for me, Doctor. It was a bad day for me, wasn't it, Mom?"

His mother giggled and winked at Dr. Pakheiser. "His birds! He think of nothing but his birds. Today he don't catch one big pheasant and this evening another get out of her house and fly away."

"Oh, I'm sorry," said the doctor. "But perhaps your bird will come back. They seem so tame. They eat out of your hand, don't they?"

"That bird won't come back," said the boy. *"I* know what happened to him. That cat got him. You get a bird tame and if it gets out anybody can catch it." The cold, accusing face began to contract in a childish pucker and tears hindered the next words: "That damned cat ate my bird!" He wrenched the mattress out of his mother's hands and flung it back onto the springs and flung himself upon it, sobbing maniacally. "And if I catch that cat, I'll kill it! I'll kill it! I'll kill it!"

The doctor flushed with embarrassment at this display, unchecked by the mother who merely stood smiling beside the bed. In time, the tantrum spent itself and Freddie lay shaking, face down on the naked bed. In the quiet, Mrs. Horvath, deceptively matter-of-fact, said, "Doctor, did you read that book by the doctor of Hitler? He say Hitler don't like women, only men? You think that true, Doctor?"

He could not chart her course, begun so remotely. He stalled, took off his glasses and put them on again. She went on. "I hate Hitler, Doctor. But I do not believe all what they say. This book I buy in the drugstore for one dollar ninety-eight cents. I think a Jew write the book out of madness for what Hitler do to Jews."

If only he could turn his leaden flesh and carry it up the stairs to his own room and lock the door upon these savages! There rest, there drink his Dubonnet, there be at home! But a score of weights held him immobile, facing the barbarous woman and he listened to her: "I hate Hitler," she repeated. "I like Jews. But if you're mad you don't all times tell the truth, isn't it? So this doctor in this book I got say Hitler like men. You know? What you think of that, Doctor?" She went on and on. Unskilled as were her thrusts, they were direct. And when at last she was finished and had dismissed him (did she, he wondered, in her marvelously malicious mind think that perhaps *he* was the "doctor of Hitler"? Or that *he* did not like women, only men?) he felt trampled upon. Actually he ached and when he got to his room, he was sure he was coming down with something. Never in all these three years had his loneliness been so acute. It sprained his whole body, buried his faculties so deeply that sensation, if it came at all, was ambiguous and incomplete. Impassively, he accepted the anonymous voices of machines: radios, motor boats, factory whistles, trains, a random bomber. They came to him thickly insulated so that, shrill or loud as they might really be, they did not penetrate his mind but lay, all of them together, in a humming mass on the threshold. His thoughts faltered like sleep-burdened eyes or attached themselves with imbecilic fixity upon one trivial object. For a long time he studied a minute fissure in the plaster of the wall beside the window. Later, he meditated intently upon the small, dispirited American flag on a pole beside the Sikorsky plant, and when at last he broke from this trance, it was only to become absorbed in the spectacle of a fouled old fish-bucket raffishly perched on a stump at the water's edge. Once, from some remote region of the house, there came the sound of a music box tinkling over a radio and at least a hundred times he stubbornly reiterated the words he knew it heralded: "PEPSI COLA HITS THE SPOT." At last, passing his hand over his cool forehead, he closed his eyes. The sounds cohered as in delirium. He could still visualize the blackbirds and fancied them to be a deathless band of flies which refused to walk upon the glass where they could be swatted. Hearing a train screaming in the station for passengers to Boston, he tried to imagine that he stood in the Bismarckgarten waiting for the yellow tram to Mannheim, but all he could see, in his mind's eye, were the shabby girls at the flowerstall deftly plucking daffodils from the pails of water. Next, he pretended that the train he heard was the express to Munich, and this time the recollections spun out effortlessly. He had gone to Salzburg once for a fortnight at the house of a classmate, a yellow-haired boy named Heine Waffenschmidt. He remembered that in the compartment there had been two soldiers on leave who had played chess the whole journey and had gladly drunk the wine offered to them by a tipsy letter-carrier on his way to Garmisch-Partenkirchen to see his tubercular daughter who was dying. The old man's blue coat glistened with age and the brass buttons on it were so tarnished that when the light fell on them they did not shine. *"Danke,* Papa," the soldiers had said. Once, at the end of a game, they stretched and yawned and told the old man what they were planning to do. "And Papa," said one of them, "what do you think? We have hired a café and ordered a keg of Löwenbräu and we'll have Scotch whisky besides." Dr. Pakheiser remembered how whenever the train stopped at a station, the pause seemed as clearly defined as a box; his eyes burned now as if he were looking up at the bright blue ceiling light. It was hard to redeem much of the two weeks in Salzburg. He had been happy, he was quite sure, and dimly he recalled a ski tournament after which he and Heine had gone to a rathskeller for *Glühwein.* There had been a troop of players on their way to Danzig and one of them, an effeminate young man, had described the jumpers he had seen that afternoon. *"Und er geht so und so und so!"* he said, gesturing with his hands. *"'Swar unglaublich wunderbar."*

The memory was flat and he rejected it. He tried to think of his patients, but could think, instead, only of his office where something was always wrong. The electricity unaccountably went off or the water ran rusty or the windows got stuck. Today Miss Johnson had worn an artificial rose in her hair and he had already been so nervous that the sight of it had nearly sent him into a tailspin.

He had a glass of brandy which quieted his fidgeting

hands. The smoke from the flat Egyptian Prettiest gave off a fragrance like sweet wood, but tonight, it did not bring back Greta. Through the open windows came sharply the sound of Mr. Horvath's voice warning his son who was clipping the hedge. "Watch out for snakes, Freddie." The shears clicked steadily; the boy was a good worker. With his glass in his hand, the doctor went to the window and stood beside it looking out. The appalling grin had come back to Freddie's face in which there were no signs of sorrow or even of anger. Once he stood up straight to rest his back from its stooping position and the big clippers dangled by their handle from his little finger.

Dr. Pakheiser went straight through the brandy and even then had not had enough to drink, so he replaced the empty decanter with the one half full of kümmel. He thought of the supper he soon would eat and he began to wonder what the Horvath family had upon their table. For some reason, he had an idea they were fond of mussels (which made him ill) and he was positive they enjoyed the displeasing flavor of celeriac in their soup. They would have chunks of fat meat; they would especially like rutabaga, watermelon, molasses, pancakes and hot tamales. Again, he wondered if they ever bathed. He had frequently seen Mrs. Horvath's wash hanging on the line in the back yard and had been certain that she used neither soap nor hot water in her laundry. He suspected that they did not brush their teeth which were very long and extremely black. He did not, to tell the truth, altogether understand why the United States had given Mr. Horvath citizenship.

The sun went down and the helicopters left the sky. At a little before seven, the doctor heard a noise in his room and, conscious that he was quite drunk, he allowed his full lips to curl into a smile as he thought of the pleasure Milenka would have if this were a mouse he might catch for his first course. The sound came again, a faint rustling. He thought at first it was in the closet, but then, at its repetition, concluded that it was in the fireplace. Rather slowly, for his hands were awkward, he took away the flowered screen and looked in at the bare, clean hearth. The sound continued, close beside him. He stuck his head in the opening and listened and it came again. There was no doubt about it, something was trapped in the chimney. He returned to his chair in indecision and poured out another glass of kümmel and considered. He knew that it was Freddie's lost bird, beating its wings against the walls.

The boy had left the hedge and his shears lay atop the formal leaves. He would be at his supper now (were they not, at this very moment, spooning up the repellent sauce that surrounded their mussels?) so there was still time in which to choose between an armistice and revenge. For a few minutes the man sat still in his rocking chair, listening tensely to the desperate wings. But presently he could endure the creature's agony no longer and he left his room, having decided to drive a bargain with the boy.

From the top of the stairs, Dr. Pakheiser could see through the window to the left of the front door. Milenka was sitting on the wall, looking archly down at the tabby who crouched in the grass. "I-yi-yi-yi, bad puss," he thought. His feet were slow on the steps and he clutched the bannister with an unnaturally moist hand. He was halfway down when Mr. Horvath came into his ken. The large man moved soundlessly around the corner of the house and stood at the edge of the lawn under a young elm tree, and in a moment, Freddie joined him, carrying a rifle. Dr. Pakheiser hesitated for the length of time it took Mr. Horvath to aim and fire and then, in order not to see the body fall off the wall, turned and went back to his room.

Late, after the Chance Vought worker had gone to the graveyard shift, Dr. Pakheiser opened the damper of the fireplace and a dead oriole fell to the hearth. He gazed abstractedly at the black and golden feathers and touched the soft body with the fire tongs. A bright apple leaf was caught under one wing. He picked the bird up carefully with a piece of newspaper and put it in a box which he found on the shelf of his closet. He carried the box downstairs and into the back yard and he floated it on the water, blue with the lights from the factory windows. He pondered if it would float to the Sound and if it did, how far it would go then. A mile on the way to Europe? Halfway? "Go, Milenka," he addressed the box which already had drifted several feet from the bank. In the cool air his head cleared a little and he felt a wonderful exhilaration as if he had been freed of a persistent pain. He ran like a young man back to the house, took the stairs two at a time and when he got to his room, he lay down without undressing and at once was fast asleep.

THE SCREAM ON FIFTY-SEVENTH STREET

Hortense Calisher

WHEN THE SCREAM came, from downstairs in the street five flights below her bedroom window, Mrs. Hazlitt, who in her month's tenancy of the flat had become the lightest of sleepers, stumbled up, groped her way past the empty second twin bed that stood nearer the window, and looked out. There was nothing to be seen of course—the apartment house she was in, though smartly kept up to the standards of the neighborhood, dated from the era of front fire escapes, and the sound, if it had come at all, had come from directly beneath them. From other half-insomniac nights she knew that the hour must be somewhere between three and four in the morning. The "all-night" doorman who guarded the huge façade of the apartment house opposite had retired, per custom, to some region behind its canopy; the one

down the block at the corner of First, who blew his
taxi-whistle so incessantly that she had for some nights
mistaken it for a traffic policeman's, had been quiet for
a long time. Even the white-shaded lamp that burned all
day and most of the night on the top floor of the little
gray town house sandwiched between the tall buildings
across the way—an invalid's light perhaps—had been
quenched. At this hour the wide expanse of the avenue,
Fifty-Seventh Street at its easternmost end, looked calm,
reassuring and amazingly silent for one of the main arter-
ies of the city. The cross-town bus service had long since
ceased; the truck traffic over on First made only an occasional dim rumble. If she went into the next room, where
there was a French window opening like a double door,
and leaned out, absurd idea, in her nightgown, she
would see, far down to the right, the lamps of a portion
of the Queensboro Bridge, quietly necklaced on the
night. In the blur beneath them, out of range but comfortable to imagine, the beautiful cul-de-sac of Sutton
Square must be musing, Edwardian in the starlight, its
one antique bow-front jutting over the river shimmering
below. And in the façades opposite her, lights were still
spotted here and there, as was always the case, even in
the small hours, in New York. Other consciousnesses
were awake, a vigil of anonymous neighbors whom she
would never know, that still gave one the hive-sense of
never being utterly alone.

All was silent. No, she must have dreamed it, reinterpreted in her doze some routine sound, perhaps the siren of the police car that often keened through this street but never stopped, no doubt on its way to the more tumultuous West Side. Until the death of her husband, companion of twenty years, eight months ago, her ability to sleep had always been healthy and immediate; since then it had gradually, not unnaturally deteriorated, but this was the worst; she had never done this before. For she could still hear very clearly the character of the sound, or rather its lack of one—a long, oddly sustained note, then a shorter one, both perfectly even, not discernible as a man's or a woman's, and without—yes, without the color of any emotion—surely the sound that one heard in dreams. Never a woman of small midnight fears in either city or country, as a girl she had done settlement work on some of this city's blackest streets, as a mining engineer's wife had nestled peacefully within the shrieking velvet of an Andes night. Not to give herself special marks for this, it was still all the more reason why what she had heard, or thought she had heard, must have been hallucinatory. A harsh word, but she must be stern with herself at the very beginnings of any such, of what could presage the sort of disintegrating widowhood, full of the mouse-fears and softening self-indulgences of the manless, that she could not, would not abide. Scarcely a second or two could have elapsed between that long—yes, that was it, soulless—cry, and her arrival at the window. And look, down there on the street and upward, everything remained motionless. Not a soul, in answer, had erupted from a doorway. All the fanlights of the lobbies shone serenely. Up above, no one leaned, not a window had flapped wide. After twenty years of living outside of the city, she could still flatter herself that she knew New York down to the ground—she had been born here, and raised. Secretly mourning it, missing it through all the happiest suburban years, she had kept up with it like a scholar, building a red-book of it for herself even through all its savage, incontinent rebuilding. She still knew all its neighborhoods. She knew. And this was one in which such a sound would be policed at once, such a cry serviced at once, if only by doormen running. No, the fault, the disturbance, must be hers.

Reaching into the pretty, built-in wardrobe on her right—the flat, with so many features that made it more like a house, fireplace, high ceilings, had attracted her from the first for this reason—she took out a warm dressing gown and sat down on the bed to put on her slippers. The window was wide open and she meant to leave it that way; country living had made unbearable the steam heat of her youth. There was no point to winter otherwise, and she—she and Sam—had always been ones to enjoy the weather as it came. Perhaps she had been unwise to give up the dog, excuse for walks early and late, outlet for talking aloud—the city was full of them. Unwise too, in the self-denuding impulse of loss, to have made herself that solitary in readiness for a city where she would have to remake friends, and no longer had kin. And charming as this flat was, wooed as she increasingly was by the delicately winning personality of its unknown, absent owner, Mrs. Berry, by her bric-a-brac, her cookbooks, even by her widowhood, almost as recent as Mrs. Hazlitt's own—perhaps it would be best to do something about getting the empty second twin bed removed from this room. No doubt Mrs. Berry, fled to London, possibly even residing in the rooms of yet a third woman in search of recommended change, would understand. Mrs. Hazlitt stretched her arms, able to smile at this imagined procession of women inhabiting each other's rooms, fallen one against the other like a pack of playing cards. How could she have forgotten what anyone who had reached middle age through the normal amount of trouble should know, that the very horizontal position itself of sleep, when one could not, laid one open to every attack from within, on a couch with no psychiatrist to listen but oneself. The best way to meet the horrors was on two feet, vertical. What she meant to do now was to fix herself a sensible hot drink, not coffee, reminiscent of shared midnight snacks, not even tea, but a nursery drink, cocoa. In a lifetime, she thought, there are probably two eras of the sleep that is utterly sound: the nursery sleep (if one had the lucky kind of childhood I did) and the sleep next or near the heart and body of the one permanently loved and loving, if one has been lucky enough for that too. I must learn from within, as well as without, that both are over. She stood up, tying her sash more firmly. And at that moment the scream came again.

She listened, rigid. It came exactly as remembered, one shrilled long note, then the shorter second, like a cut-off Amen to the first and of the same timbre, dreadful in its cool, a madness expanded almost with calm, near the edge of joy. No wonder she had thought of the siren; this had the same note of terror controlled. One could not tell whether it sped toward a victim or from one. As before, it seemed to come from directly below.

Shaking, she leaned out, could see nothing because of the high sill, ran into the next room, opened the French window and all but stood on the fire escape. As she did so, the sound, certainly human, had just ceased; at the same moment a cab, going slowly down the middle of the avenue, its toplight up, veered directly toward her, as if the driver too had heard, poised there beneath her with its nose pointed toward the curb, then veered sharply back to the center of the street, gathered speed, and drove on. Immediately behind it another cab, toplight off, slowed up, performed exactly the same orbit, then it too, with a hasty squeal of brakes, made for the center street and sped away. In the confusion of noises she thought she heard the grind of a window-sash coming down, then a slam—perhaps the downstairs door of the adjoining set of flats, or of this one. Dropping to her knees, she leaned both palms on the floor-level lintel of the window and peered down through the iron slats of her fire escape and the successive ones below. Crouched that way, she could see straight back to the building line. To the left, a streetlamp cast a pale, even glow on empty sidewalk and the free space of curb either side of a hydrant; to the right, the shadows were obscure, but motionless. She saw nothing to conjure into a half-expected human bundle lying still, heard no footfall staggering or slipping away. Not more than a minute or two could have elapsed since she had heard the cry. Tilting her head up at the façades opposite, she saw that their simple pattern of lit windows seemed the same. While she stared, one of the squares blotted out, then another, both on floors not too high to have heard. Would no one, having heard, attend? Would she?

Standing up, her hand on the hasp of the French window, she felt herself still shaking, not with fear, but with the effort to keep herself from in some way heeding that cry. Again she told herself that she had been born here, knew the city's ways, had not the *auslander's* incredulity about some of them. These ways had hardened since her day, people had warned her, to an indifference beyond that of any civilized city; there were no "good" neighborhoods now, none of any kind really, except the half-hostile enclosure that each family must build for itself. She had discounted this, knowing unsentimentally what city life was; even in the tender version of it that was her childhood there had been noises, human ones, that the most responsible people, the kindest, had shrugged away, saying, "Nothing, dear. Something outside." What she had not taken into account was her own twenty years of living elsewhere, where such a cry in the night would be succored at once if only for gossip's sake, if only because one gave up privacy—anonymity—forever, when one went to live in a house on a road. If only, she thought, holding herself rigid to stop her trembling, because it would be the cry of someone one knew. Nevertheless, it took all her strength not to rush downstairs, to hang on to the handle, while in her mind's eye she ran out of her apartment door, remembering to take the key, pressed the elevator button and waited, went down at the car's deliberate pace. After that there would be the inner, buzzer door to open, then at last the door to the outside. No, it would take too long, and it was already too late for the phone, by the time police could come or she could find the number of the superintendent in his back basement—and when either answered, what would she say? She looked at the fire escape. Not counting hers, there must be three others between herself and the street. Whether there was a ladder extending from the lowest one she could not remember; possibly one hung by one's hands and dropped to the ground. Years ago there had been more of them, even the better houses had had them in their rear areaways, but she had never in her life seen one used. And this one fronted direct on the avenue. It was this that brought her to her senses—the vision of herself in her blue robe creeping down the front of a building on Fifty-Seventh Street, hanging by her hands until she dropped to the ground. She shut the long window quickly, leaning her weight against it to help the slightly swollen frame into place, and turned the handle counterclockwise, shooting the long vertical bolt. The bolt fell into place with a thump she had never noticed before but already seemed familiar. Probably, she thought, sighing, it was the kind of sound—old hardware on old wood—that more often went with a house.

In the kitchen, over her cocoa, she shook herself with a reminiscent tremble, in the way one did after a narrow escape. It was a gesture made more often to a companion, an auditor. Easy enough to make the larger gestures involved in cutting down one's life to the pattern of the single; the selling of a house, the arranging of income or new occupation. Even the abnegation of sex had a drama that lent one strength, made one hold up one's head as one saw oneself traveling a clear, melancholy line. It was the small gestures for which there was no possible sublimation, the sudden phrase, posture—to no auditor, the constant clueing of identity in another's—its cessation. "Dear me," she would have said—they would have come to town for the winter months as they had often planned, and he would have just returned from an overnight business trip—"what do you suppose I'd have done, Sam, if I'd gone all the way, in my housecoat, really found myself outside? Funny how the distinction between outdoors and in breaks down in the country. I'd forgotten how absolute it is here—with so many barriers between." Of course, she thought, that's the simple reason why here, in the city, the sense of responsibility has to weaken. Who could maintain it, through a door, an elevator, a door and a door, toward everyone, anyone, who screamed? Perhaps that was the real reason she had come here, she thought, washing the cup under the faucet. Where the walls are soundproofed there are no more "people next door" with their ready "casserole" pity, at worst with the harbored glow of their own family life peering from their averted eyelids like the lamplight from under their eaves. Perhaps she had known all along that the best way to learn how to live alone was to come to the place where people really were.

She set the cup out for the morning and added a plate and a spoon. It was wiser not to let herself deteriorate to the utterly casual; besides, the sight of them always gave her a certain pleasure, like a greeting, if only from herself of the night before. Tomorrow she had a meeting, of one of the two hospital boards on which, luckily for now, she had served for years. There was plenty more of that kind of useful occupation available and no one would care a hoot whether what once she had done for conscience' sake she now did for her own. The meeting was not scheduled until two. Before that she would manage to inquire very discreetly, careful not to appear either eccentric or too friendly, both of which made city people uneasy, as to whether anyone else in the building had heard what she had. This too she would do for discipline's sake. There was no longer any doubt that the sound had been real.

The next morning at eight-thirty, dressed to go out except for her coat, she waited just inside her door for one or the other of the tenants on her floor to emerge. Her heart pounded at the very queerness of what she was doing, but she overruled it; if she did feel somewhat too interested, too much as if she were embarking on a chase, then let her get it out of her system at once, and have done. How to do so was precisely what she had considered while dressing. The problem was not to make too many inquiries, too earnest ones, and not to seem to be making any personal overture, from which people would naturally withdraw. One did not make inconvenient, hothouse friendships in the place one lived in, here. Therefore she had decided to limit her approaches to three—the first to the girl who lived in the adjacent apartment, who could usually be encountered at this hour and was the only tenant she knew for sure lived in the front of the building—back tenants were less likely to have heard. For the rest, she must trust to luck. And whatever the outcome, she would not let herself pursue the matter beyond today.

She opened the door a crack and listened. Still too early. Actually the place, being small—six floors of four or five flats each—had a more intimate feeling than most. According to the super's wife, Mrs. Stump, with whom she had had a chat or two in the hall, many of the tenants, clinging to ceiling rents in what had become a fancier district, had been here for years, a few for the thirty since the place had been built. This would account for so many middle-aged and elderly, seemingly either single or the remnants of families—besides various quiet, well-mannered women who, like herself, did not work, she had noticed at times two men who were obviously father and son, two others who, from their ages and nameplate, noticed at mailtime, might be brothers, and a mother with the only child in the place—a subdued little girl of about eight. As soon as a tenant of long standing vacated or died, Mrs. Stump had added, the larger units were converted to smaller, and this would account for the substratum of slightly showier or younger occupants: two modish blondes, a couple of homburged "decorator" types—all more in keeping with the newly sub-theatrical,

antique-shop character of the neighborhood—as well as
for the "career girl" on her floor. Mrs. Berry, who from
evidences in the flat should be something past forty like
herself, belonged to the first group, having been here,
with her husband of course until recently, since just after
the war. A pity that she, Mrs. Berry, who from her books,
her one charming letter, her own situation, might have
been just the person to understand, even share Mrs. Hazlitt's reaction to the event of last night, was not here. But
this was nonsense; if she were, then she, Mrs. Hazlitt,
would not be. She thought again of the chain of women,
sighed, and immediately chid herself for this new habit
of sighing, as well as for this alarming mound of gratui-
tous information she seemed to have acquired, in less
than a month, about people with whom she was in no way
concerned. At that moment she heard the door next hers
creak open. Quickly she put on her coat, opened her
door and bent to pick up the morning paper. The girl
coming out stepped back, dropping one of a pile of boxes
she was carrying. Mrs. Hazlitt returned it to her, pressed
the button for the elevator, and when it came, held the
door. It was the girl she had seen twice before; for the
first time they had a nice exchange of smiles.

"Whoops, I'm late," said the girl, craning to look at
her watch.

"Me too," said Mrs. Hazlitt, as the cage slid slowly
down. She drew breath. "Overslept, once I did get to

sleep. Rather a noisy night outside—did you hear all that fuss, must have been around three or four?" She waited hopefully for the answer: Why yes indeed, what on earth was it, did you?

"Uh-uh," said the girl, shaking her head serenely. "'Fraid the three of us sleep like a log, that's the trouble. My roommates are still at it, lucky stiffs." She checked her watch again, was first out of the elevator, nodded her thanks when Mrs. Hazlitt hurried to hold the buzzer door for her because of the boxes, managed the outer door herself, and departed.

Mrs. Hazlitt walked briskly around the corner to the bakery, came back with her bag of two brioches, and reentered. Imagine, there are three of them, she thought, and I never knew. Well, I envy them their log. The inner door, usually locked, was propped open. Mrs. Stump was on her knees just behind it, washing the marble floor, as she did every day. It was certainly a tidy house, not luxurious but up to a firmly well-bred standard, just the sort a woman like Mrs. Berry would have, that she herself, when the sublease was over, would like to find. Nodding to Mrs. Stump, she went past her to the row of brass mail slots, pretending to search her own although she knew it was too early, weighing whether she ought to risk wasting one of her three chances on her.

"Mail don't come till ten," said Mrs. Stump from behind her.

"Yes, I know," said Mrs. Hazlitt, recalling suddenly that they had had this exchange before. "But I forgot to check yesterday."

"Yesterday vass holiday."

"Oh, so it was." Guiltily Mrs. Hazlitt entered the elevator and faced the door, relieved when it closed. The truth was that she had known yesterday was a holiday and had checked the mail anyway. The truth was that she often did this even on Sundays here, often even more than once. It made an errand in the long expanse of a day when she either flinched from the daily walk that was too dreary to do alone on Sunday, or had not provided herself with a ticket to something. One had to tidy one's hair, spruce a bit for the possible regard of someone in the hall, and when she did see someone, although of course they never spoke, she always returned feeling refreshed, reaffirmed.

Upstairs again, she felt that way now; her day had begun in the eyes of others, as a day should. She made a few phone calls to laundry and bank, and felt even better. Curious how, when one lived alone, one began to feel that only one's own consciousness held up the world, and at the very same time that only an incursion into the world, or a recognition from it, made one continue to exist at all. There was another phone call she might make, to a friend up in the country, who had broken an ankle, but she would save that for a time when she needed it more. This was yet another discipline—not to become a phone bore. The era when she herself had been a victim of such, had often thought of the phone as a nuisance, now seemed as distant as China. She looked at the clock —time enough to make another pot of coffee. With it she ate a brioche slowly, then with the pleasant sense of hurry she now had so seldom, another.

At ten sharp she went downstairs again, resolving to take her chance with whoever might be there. As she emerged from the elevator she saw that she was in luck; the owner of a big brown poodle—a tall, well set up man of sixty or so—was bent over his mail slot while the dog stood by. It was the simplest of matters to make an over-ture to the poodle, who was already politely nosing the palm she offered him, to expose her own love of the breed, remarking on this one's exceptional manners, to skip lightly on from the question of barking to noise in general, to a particular noise.

"Ah well, Coco's had stage training," said his owner, in answer to her compliments. She guessed that his owner might have had the same; he had that fine, bravura face which aging actors of another generation often had, a trifle shallow for its years perhaps but very fine, and he inclined toward her with the same majestic politeness as his dog, looking into her face very intently as she spoke, answering her in the slender, semi-British accent she recalled from matinee idols of her youth. She had to repeat her question on the noise. This time she firmly gave the sound its name—a scream, really rather an unusual scream.

"A scream?" The man straightened. She thought that for a moment he looked dismayed. Then he pursed his lips very judiciously, in almost an acting-out of that kind of repose. "Come to think of it, ye-es, I may have heard something." He squared his shoulders. "But no doubt I just turned over. And Coco's a city dog, very blasé fellow. Rather imagine he did too." He tipped his excellent homburg. "Good morning," he added, with sudden reserve, and turned away, giving a flick to the dog's leash that started the animal off with his master behind him.

"Good morning," she called after them, "and thanks for the tip on where to get one like Coco." Coco looked back at her; but his master, back turned, disentangling the leash from the doorknob, did not, and went out without answering.

So I've done it after all, she thought. Too friendly. Especially too friendly since I'm a woman. Her face grew hot at this probable estimate of her—gushy woman chattering over-brightly, lingering in the hall. Bore of a woman who heard things at night, no doubt looked under the bed before she got into it. No, she thought, there was something—when I mentioned the scream. At the aural memory of that latter, still clear, she felt her resolve stiffen. Also—what a dunce she was being—there were the taxis. Taxis, one of them occupied, did not veer, one after the other, on an empty street, without reason. Emboldened, she bent to look at the man's mailbox. The name, Reginald Warwick, certainly fitted her imaginary dossier, but that was not what gave her pause. Apartment 3A. Hers was 5A. He lived in the front, two floors beneath her, where he must have heard.

As she inserted the key in her apartment door, she heard the telephone ringing, fumbled the key and dropped it, then had to open the double lock up above. All part of the city picture, she thought resentfully, remembering their four doors, never locked, in the country—utterly foolhardy, never to be dreamed of here. Even if she had, there were Mrs. Berry's possessions to be considered, nothing extraordinary, but rather like the modest, crotchety bits of treasure she had inherited or acquired herself—in the matter of bric-a-brac alone there was really quite a kinship between them. The phone was still ringing as she entered. She raced toward it eagerly. It was the secretary of the hospital board, telling her that this afternoon's meeting was put off.

"Oh . . . oh dear," said Mrs. Hazlitt. "I mean—I'm so sorry to hear about Mrs. Levin. Hope it's nothing serious."

"I really couldn't say," said the secretary. "But we've enough for a quorum the week after." She rang off.

Mrs. Hazlitt put down the phone, alarmed at the sudden sinking of her heart over such a minor reversal. She had looked forward to seeing people of course, but particularly to spending an afternoon in the brightly capable impersonality of the boardroom, among men and women who brought with them a sense of indefinable swathes of well-being extending behind them, of such a superfluity of it, from lives as full as their checkbooks, that they were met in that efficient room to dispense what overflowed. The meeting would have been an antidote to that dark, anarchic version of the city which had been obsessing her; it would have been a reminder that everywhere, on flight after flight of the city's high, brilliant floors, similar groups of the responsible were convening, could always be applied to, were in command. The phone gave a reminiscent tinkle as she pushed it aside, and she waited, but there was no further ring. She looked at her calendar, scribbled with domestic markings—the hairdresser on Tuesday, a fitting for her spring suit, the date when she must appear at the lawyer's for the closing on the sale of the house. Beyond that she had a dinner party with old acquaintances on the following Thursday, tickets with a woman friend for the Philharmonic on Saturday week. Certainly she was not destitute of either company or activity. But the facts were that within the next two weeks, she could look forward to only two occasions when she would be communicating on any terms of intimacy with people who, within limits, knew "who" she was. A default on either would be felt keenly—much more than the collapse of this afternoon's little—prop. Absently she twiddled the dial back and forth. Proportion was what went first "in solitary"; circling one's own small platform in space, the need for speech mute in one's own throat, one developed an abnormal concern over the night-cries of others. No, she thought, remembering the board meeting, those high convocations of the responsible, I've promised—Lord knows who, myself, somebody. She stood up and gave herself a smart slap on the buttock. "Come on, Millie," she said, using the nickname her husband always had. "Get on with it." She started to leave the room, then remained in its center, hand at her mouth, wondering. Talking aloud to oneself was more common than admitted; almost everyone did. It was merely that she could not decide whether or not she had.

Around eleven o'clock, making up a bundle of lingerie, she went down to the basement where there was a community washing machine, set the machine's cycle, and went back upstairs. Forty minutes later she went through the same routine, shifting the wet clothes to the dryer. At one o'clock she returned for the finished clothes and carried them up. This made six trips in all, but at no time had she met anyone en route; it was Saturday afternoon, perhaps a bad time. At two she went out to do her weekend shopping. The streets were buzzing, the women in the supermarket evidently laying in enough stores for a visitation of giants. Outside the market, a few kids from Third Avenue always waited in the hope of tips for carrying, and on impulse, although her load was small, she engaged a boy of about ten. On the way home, promising him extra for waiting, she stopped at the patisserie where she always lingered for the sheer gilt-and-chocolate gaiety of the place, bought her brioches for the morning, and, again on impulse, an éclair for the boy. Going up in the elevator they encountered the mother and small girl, but she had never found any pretext for addressing that glum pair, the mother engaged as usual in a low, toneless tongue-lashing of the child. Divorcée, Mrs. Hazlitt fancied, and no man in the offing, an inconvenient child. In the kitchen, she tipped the boy and offered him the pastry. After an astonished glance, he wolfed it with a practical air, peering at her furtively between bites, and darted off at once, looking askance over his shoulder at her. "See you next Saturday, maybe." Obviously he had been brought up to believe that only witches dispensed free gingerbread. In front of the bathroom mirror, Mrs. Hazlitt, tidying up before her walk, almost ritual now, to Sutton Square, regarded her image, not yet a witch's but certainly a fool's, a country-cookie-jar fool's. "Oh well, you're company," she said, quite consciously aloud this time, and for some reason this cheered her. Before leaving, she went over face and costume with the laborious attention she always gave them nowadays before going anywhere outside.

Again, when she rode down, she met no one, but she walked with bracing step, making herself take a circuitous route for health's sake, all the way to Bloomingdale's, then on to Park and around again, along the Fifty-Eighth Street bridge pass, the dejectedly frivolous shops that lurked near it, before she let herself approach the house with the niche with the little statue of Dante in it, then the Square. Sitting in the Square, the air rapidly blueing now, lapping her like reverie, she wondered whether any of the residents of the windows surrounding her had noticed her almost daily presence, half hoped they had. Before it became too much of a habit, of course, she would stop coming. Meanwhile, if she took off her distance glasses, the scene before her, seen through the tender, Whistlerian blur of myopia—misted gray bridge, blue and green lights of a barge going at its tranced pace downriver—was the very likeness of a corner of the Chelsea embankment, glimpsed throughout a winter of happy teatime windows seven years ago, from a certain angle below Battersea Bridge. Surely it was blameless to remember past happiness if one did so without self-pity, better still, of course, to be able to speak of it to someone in an even, healing voice. Idly she wondered where Mrs. Berry was living in London. The flat in Cheyne Walk would have just suited her. "Just the

thing for you," she would have said to her had she
known her. "The Sebrings still let it every season. We
always meant to go back." Her watch said five and the
air was chilling. She walked rapidly home through the
evening scurry, the hour of appointments, catching its
excitement as she too hurried, half-persuaded of her own
appointment, mythical but still possible, with someone as
yet unknown. Outside her own building she paused. All
day long she had been entering it from the westerly side.
Now, approaching from the east, she saw that the fire
escape on this side of the entrance did end in a ladder,
about four feet above her. Anyone moderately tall, like
herself, would have had an easy drop of it, as she would
have done last night. Shaking her head at that crazy
image, she looked up at the brilliant hives all around her.
Lights were cramming in, crowding on, but she knew too
much now about their nighttime progression, their grad-
ual decline to a single indifferent string on that rising,
insomniac silence in which she might lie until morning,
dreading to hear again what no one else would appear to
have heard. Scaring myself to death, she thought (or
muttered?), and in the same instant resolved to drop all
limits, go down to the basement and interrogate the
Stumps, sit on the bench in the lobby and accost anyone
who came in, ring doorbells if necessary, until she had
confirmation—and not go upstairs until she had. "Excuse
me," said someone. She turned. A small, frail, elderly

woman, smiling timidly, waited to get past her through the outer door.

"Oh—sorry," said Mrs. Hazlitt. "Why—good evening!" she added with a rush, an enormous rush of relief. "Here—let me," she said more quietly, opening the door with a numb sense of gratitude for having been tugged back from the brink of what she saw now, at the touch of a voice, had been panic. For here was a tenant, unaccountably forgotten, with whom she was almost on speaking terms, a gentle old sort, badly crippled with arthritis, for whom Mrs. Hazlitt had once or twice unlocked the inner door. She did so now.

"Thank you, my dear—my hands are that knobbly." There was the trace of brogue that Mrs. Hazlitt had noticed before. The old woman, her gray hair sparse from the disease but freshly done in the artfully messy arrangements used to conceal the skulls of old ladies, her broadtail coat not new but excellently maintained, gave off the comfortable essence, pleasing as rosewater, of one who had been serenely protected all her life. Unmarried, for she had that strangely deducible aura about her even before one noted the lack of ring, she had also a certain simpleness, now almost bygone, of those household women who had never gone to business—Mrs. Hazlitt had put her down as perhaps the relict sister of a contractor, or of a school superintendent of the days when the system had been Irish from top to bottom, at the top, of

Irish of just this class. The old lady fumbled now with the minute key to her mailbox.

"May I?"

"Ah, if you would now. Couldn't manage it when I came down. The fingers don't seem to warm up until evening. It's 2B."

Mrs. Hazlitt, inserting the key, barely noticed the name—Finan. 2B would be a front apartment also, in the line adjacent to the A's.

"And you would be the lady in Mrs. Berry's. Such a nicely spoken woman, she was."

"Oh yes, isn't she," said Mrs. Hazlitt. "I mean . . . I just came through the agent. But when you live in a person's house—do you know her?"

"Just to speak. Half as long as me, they'd lived here. Fifteen years." The old lady took the one letter Mrs. Hazlitt passed her, the yellow-fronted rent bill whose duplicate she herself had received this morning. "Ah well, we're always sure of this one, aren't we?" Nodding her thanks, she shuffled toward the elevator on built-up shoes shaped like hods. "Still, it's a nice, quiet building, and lucky we are to be in it these days."

There was such a rickety bravery about her, of neat habit long overborne by the imprecisions of age, of dowager hat set slightly askew by fingers unable to deal with a key yet living alone, that Mrs. Hazlitt, reluctant to shake the poor, tottery dear further, had to remind herself of the moment before their encounter.

"Last night?" The old blue eyes looked blank, then brightened. "Ah no, I must have taken one of my Seconals. Otherwise I'd have heard it surely. 'Auntie,' my niece always says—'what if there should be a fire, and you there sleeping away?' Do what she says, I do sometimes, only to hear every pin drop till morning." She shook her head, entering the elevator. "Going up?"

"N-no," said Mrs. Hazlitt. "I—have to wait here for a minute." She sat down on the bench, the token bench that she had never seen anybody sitting on, and watched the car door close on the little figure still shaking its head, borne upward like a fairy godmother, willing but unable to oblige. The car's hum stopped, then its light glowed on again. Someone else was coming down. No, this is the nadir, Mrs. Hazlitt thought. Whether I heard it or not, I'm obviously no longer myself. Sleeping pills for me too, though I've never—and no more nonsense. And no more questioning, no matter who.

The car door opened. "Wssht!" said Miss Finan, scuttling out again. "I've just remembered. Not last night, but two weeks ago. And once before that. A scream, you said?"

Mrs. Hazlitt stood up. Almost unable to speak, for the tears that suddenly wrenched her throat, she described it.

"That's it, just what I told my niece on the phone next morning. Like nothing human, and yet it was. I'd taken my Seconal too early, so there I was wide awake again, lying there just thinking, when it came. 'Auntie,' she tried to tell me, 'it was just one of the sireens. Or hoodlums maybe.' " Miss Finan reached up very slowly and settled her hat. "The city's gone down, you know. Not what it was," she said in a reduced voice, casting a glance over her shoulder, as if whatever the city now was loomed behind her. "But I've laid awake on this street too many years, I said, not to know what I hear." She leaned forward. "But—she . . . they think I'm getting old, you know," she said, in the whisper used to confide the unimaginable. "So . . . well . . . when I heard it again I just didn't tell her."

Mrs. Hazlitt grubbed for her handkerchief, found it and blew her nose. Breaking down, she thought—I never knew what a literal phrase it is. For she felt as if all the muscles that usually held her up, knee to ankle, had slipped their knots and were melting her, unless she could stop them, to the floor. "I'm not normally such a nervous woman," she managed to say. "But it was just that no one else seemed to—why, there were people with lights on, but they just seemed to ignore."

The old lady nodded absently. "Well, thank God my hearing's as good as ever. Hmm. Wait till I tell Jennie that!" She began making her painful way back to the car.

Mrs. Hazlitt put out a hand to delay her. "In case it— I mean, in case somebody ought to be notified—do you have any idea what it was?"

"Oh, I don't know. And what could we—?" Miss

Finan shrugged, eager to get along. Still, gossip was tempting. "I did think—" She paused, lowering her voice uneasily. "Like somebody in a fit, it was. We'd a sexton at church taken that way with epilepsy once. And it stopped short like that, just as if somebody'd clapped a hand over its mouth, poor devil. Then the next time I thought—no, more like a signal, like somebody calling. You know the things you'll think at night." She turned, clearly eager to get away.

"But, oughtn't we to inquire?" Mrs. Hazlitt thought of the taxis. "In case it came from this building?"

"This build—" For a moment Miss Finan looked scared, her chin trembling, eyes rounded in the misty, affronted stare that the old gave, not to physical danger, but to a new idea swum too late into their ken. Then she drew herself up, all five feet of her bowed backbone. "Not from here it wouldn't. Across from that big place, maybe. Lots of riffraff there, not used to their money. Or from Third Avenue, maybe. That's always been tenements there." She looked at Mrs. Hazlitt with an obtuse patronage that reminded her of an old nurse who had first instructed her on the social order, blandly mixing up all first causes—disease, money, poverty, snobbery— with a firm illogic that had still seemed somehow in possession—far more firmly so than her own good-hearted parents—of the crude facts. "New to the city, are you," she said, more kindly. "It takes a while."

This time they rode up together. "Now you remember," Miss Finan said, on leaving. "You've two locks on your door, one downstairs. Get a telephone put in by your bed. Snug as a bug in a rug you are then. Nothing to get at you but what's there already. That's what I always tell myself when I'm wakeful. Nothing to get at you then but the Old Nick."

The door closed on her. Watching her go, Mrs. Hazlitt envied her the simplicity, even the spinsterhood that had barred her from imagination as it had from experience. Even the narrowing-in of age would have its compensations, tenderly constricting the horizon as it cramped the fingers, adding the best of locks to Miss Finan's snugness, on her way by now to the triumphant phone call to Jennie.

But that was sinful, to wish for that too soon, what's more it was sentimental, in just the way she had vowed to avoid. Mrs. Hazlitt pushed the button for Down. Emerging from the building, she looked back at it from the corner, back at her day of contrived exits and entrances, abortive conversations. People were hurrying in and out now at a great rate. An invisible glass separated her from them; she was no longer in the fold.

Later that night, Mrs. Hazlitt, once more preparing for bed, peered down at the streets through the slats of the Venetian blind. Catching herself in the attitude of peering made her uneasy. Darkening the room behind her, she raised the blind. After dinner in one of the good French restaurants on Third Avenue and a Tati movie afterward—the French were such competent dispensers of gaiety—she could review her day more as a convalescent does his delirium—"Did I really say—do—that?" And even here she was addressing a vis-à-vis, so deeply was the habit ingrained. But she could see her self-imposed project now for what it was—only a hysterical seeking after conversation, the final breaking-point, like the old-fashioned "crisis" in pneumonia, of the long, low fever of loneliness unexpressed. Even the city, gazed at squarely, was really no anarchy, only a huge diffuseness that returned to the eye of the beholder, to the walker in its streets, even to the closed dream of its sleeper, his own mood, dark or light. Dozens of the solitary must be looking down at it with her, most of them with some *modus vivendi,* many of them booking themselves into life with the same painful intentness, the way the middle-aged sometimes set themselves to learning the tango. And a queer booking you gave yourself today, she told herself, the words lilting with Miss Finan's Irish, this being the last exchange of speech she had had. Testing the words aloud, she found her way with accents, always such a delight to Sam, as good as ever. Well, she had heard a scream, had discovered someone else who had heard it. And now to forget it as promised; the day was done. Prowling the room a bit, she took up her robe, draped it over her shoulders, still more providently put it on. "Oh Millie," she said, tossing the dark mirror a look of scorn as she passed it, "you're such a sensible woman."

Wear out Mrs. Berry's carpet you will, Millie, she thought, twenty minutes later by the bedroom clock, but the accent, adulterated now by Sam's, had escaped her. Had the scream had an accent? The trouble was that the mind had its own discipline; one could remember, even with a smile, the story of the man promised all the gold in the world if he could but go for two minutes not thinking of the word "hippopotamus." She stopped in front of the mirror, seeking her smile, but it too had escaped. "Hippopotamus," she said, to her dark image. The knuckles of one hand rose, somnambulist, as she watched, and pressed against her teeth. She forced the hand, hers, down again. I will say it again, aloud, she thought, and while I am saying it I will be sure to say to myself that I am saying it aloud. She did so. "Hippopotamus." For a long moment she remained there, staring into the mirror. Then she turned and snapped on every light in the room.

Across from her, in another mirror, the full-length one, herself regarded her. She went forward to it, to that image so irritatingly familiar, so constant as life changed it, so necessarily dear. Fair hair, if maintained too late in life, too brightly, always made the most sensible of women look foolish. There was hers, allowed to gray gently, disordered no more than was natural in the boudoir, framing a face still rational, if strained. "Dear me," she said to it. "All you need is somebody to talk to, get it out of your system. Somebody like yourself." As if prodded, she turned and surveyed the room.

Even in the glare of the lights, the naked black projected from the window, the room sent out to her, in half a dozen pleasant little touches, the same sense of its compatible owner that she had had from the beginning. There, flung down, was Mrs. Berry's copy of *The Eustace Diamonds,* a book that she had always meant to read and had been delighted to find here, along with many others of its ilk and still others she herself owned. How many people knew good bisque and how cheaply it might still be collected, or could let it hobnob so amiably with grandmotherly bits of Tiffanyware, even with the chipped Quimper ashtrays that Mrs. Berry, like Mrs. Hazlitt at the time of her own marriage, must once have thought the cutest in the world. There were the white walls, with the silly, strawberry-mouthed Marie Laurencin just above the Beerbohm, the presence of good faded colors, the absence of the new or fauve. On the night table were the scissors, placed, like everything in the house, where Mrs. Hazlitt would have had them, near them a relic that winked of her own childhood—and kept on, she would wager, for the same reason—a magnifying glass exactly like her father's. Above them, the only floor lamp in the house, least offensive of its kind, towered above all the table ones, sign of a struggle between practicality and grace that she knew well, whose end she could applaud. Everywhere indeed there were the same signs of the struggles toward taste, the decline of taste into the prejudices of comfort, that went with a whole milieu and a generation—both hers. And over there was, even more personally, the second bed.

Mrs. Hazlitt sat down on it. If it were moved, into the study say, a few things out of storage with it, how sympathetically this flat might be shared. Nonsense, sheer fantasy to go on like this, to fancy herself embarking on the pitiable twin-life of leftover women, much less with a stranger. But was a woman a stranger if you happened to know that on her twelfth birthday she had received a copy of *Dr. Doolittle,* inscribed to Helena Nelson from her loving father, if you knew the secret, packrat place in the linen closet where she stuffed the neglected mending, of another, in a kitchen drawer, full of broken Mexican terrines and clipped recipes as shamefully grimy as your own cherished ones; if you knew that on 2/11/58 and on 7/25/57 a Dr. Burke had prescribed what looked to be sulfa pills, never used, that must have cured her at the point of purchase, as had embarrassingly happened time and again to yourself? If, in short, you knew almost every endearing thing about her, except her face?

Mrs. Hazlitt, blinking in the excessive light, looked sideways. She knew where there was a photograph album, tumbled once by accident from its shunted place in the bookshelf, and at once honorably replaced. She had seen enough to know that the snapshots, not pasted in separately, would have to be exhumed, one by one, from their packets. No, she told herself, she already knew more than enough of Mrs. Berry from all that had been so trustfully exposed here—enough to know that this was the sort of prying to which Mrs. Berry, like herself, would never stoop. Somehow this clinched it— their understanding. She could see them exchanging notes at some future meeting, Mrs. Berry saying, "Why, do you know—one night, when I was in London—" —herself, the vis-à-vis, nodding, their perfect rapprochement. Then what would be wrong in using, when so handily provided, so graciously awaiting her, such a comforting vis-à-vis, now?

Mrs. Hazlitt found herself standing, the room's glare pressing on her as if she were arraigned in a police line-up, as if, she reminded herself irritably, it were not self-imposed. She forced herself to make a circuit of the room, turning out each lamp with the crisp, no-nonsense flick of the wrist that nurses employed. At the one lamp still burning she hesitated, reluctant to cross over that last shadowline. Then, with a shrug, she turned it out and sat down in the darkness, in one of the two opposing boudoir chairs. For long minutes she sat there. Once or twice she trembled on the verge of speech, covered it with a swallow. The conventions that guarded the mind in its strict relationship with the tongue were the hardest to flaunt. But this was the century of talk, of the long talk, in which all were healthily urged to confide. Even the children were encouraged toward, praised for, the imaginary companion. Why should the grown person, who for circumstance beyond his control had no other, be denied? As she watched the window, the light in the small gray house was extinguished. Some minutes later the doorman across the way disappeared. Without looking at the luminous dial of the clock, she could feel the silence aging, ripening. At last she bent forward to the opposite chair.

"Helena?" she said.

Her voice, clear-cut, surprised her. There was nothing so strange about it. The walls remained walls. No one could hear her, or cared to, and now, tucking her feet up, she could remember how cozy this could be, with someone opposite. "Helena," she said. "Wait till I tell you what happened while you were away."

She told her everything. At first she stumbled, went back, as if she were rehearsing in front of a mirror. Several times she froze, unsure whether a sentence had been spoken aloud entirely, or had begun, or terminated, unspoken, in the mind. But as she went on, this wavering borderline seemed only to resemble the clued conversation, meshed with silences, between two people who knew each other well. By the time she had finished her account she was almost at ease, settling back into the comfortably shared midnight post-mortem that always restored balance to the world—so nearly could she imagine the face, not unlike her own, in the chair opposite, smiling ruefully at her over the boy and his gingerbread fears, wondering mischievously with her as to in which of the shapes of temptation the Old Nick visited Miss Finan.

"That girl and her *log!*" said Mrs. Hazlitt. "You know how, when they're that young, you want to smash in the smugness. And yet, when you think of all they've got to go through, you feel so maternal. Even if—" Even if, came the nod, imperceptibly—you've never had children, like us.

For a while they were silent. "Warwick!" said Mrs. Hazlitt then. "Years ago there was an actor—Robert Warwick. I was in love with him—at about the age of eight." Then she smiled, bridling slightly, at the dark chair opposite, whose occupant would know her age. "Oh, all right then—twelve. But what is it, do you suppose, always makes old actors look seedy, even when they're not? Daylight maybe. Or all the pretenses." She ruminated. "Why . . . do you know," she said slowly, "I think I've got it. The way he looked in my face when I was speaking, and the way the dog turned back and he didn't. He was lip-reading. Why, the poor old boy is deaf!" She settled back, dropping her slippers one by one to the floor. "Of course, that's it. And he wouldn't want to admit that he couldn't have heard it. Probably doesn't dare wear an aid. Poor old boy, pretty dreary for him if he is an actor, and I'll bet he is." She sighed, a luxury permitted now. "Ah, well. Frail reed—Miss Finan. Lucky for me, though, that I stumbled on her." And on you.

A police siren sounded, muffled less and less by distance, approaching. She was at the window in time to see the car's red dome light streak by as it always did, its alarum dying behind it. Nothing else was on the road. "And there were the taxis," she said, looking down. "I don't know why I keep forgetting them. Veering to the side like that, one right after the other, and one had his light out, so it wasn't for a fare. Nothing on the curb either. Then they both shot away, almost as if they'd caught sight of something up here. And wanted no part of it—the way people do in this town. Wish you could've seen them—it was eerie." There was no response from behind her.

She sat down again. Yes, there was a response, for the first time faintly contrary.

"No," she said. "It certainly was *not* the siren. I was up in a flash. I'd have seen it." She found herself clenching the arms of the chair. "Besides," she said, in a quieter voice, "don't you remember? I heard it twice."

There was no answer. Glancing sideways, she saw the string of lights opposite, not quite of last night's pattern. But the silence was the same, opened to its perfect hour like a century plant, multiple-rooted, that came of age every night. The silence was in full bloom, and it had its own sound. Hark hark, no dogs do bark. And there is nobody in the chair.

Never was, never had been. It was sad to be up at this hour and sane. For now is the hour, now is the hour when all good men are asleep. Her hand smoothed the rim of the wastebasket, about the height from the floor of a dog's collar. Get one tomorrow. But how to manage until then, with all this silence speaking?

She made herself stretch out on the bed, close her eyes. "Sam," she said at last, as she had sworn never to do in thought or word, "I'm lonely." Listening vainly, she thought how wise her resolve had been. Too late, now she had tested his loss to the full, knew him for the void he was—far more of a one than Mrs. Berry, who, though unknown, was still somewhere. By using the name of love, when she had been ready to settle for anybody, she had sent him into the void forever. Opening her eyes, adjusted now to the sourceless city light that never ceased trickling on ceiling, lancing from mirrors, she turned her head right to left, left to right on the pillow, in a gesture to the one auditor who remained.

"No," she said, in the dry voice of correction. "I'm not lonely. I'm alone."

Almost at once she raised herself on her elbow, her head cocked. No, she had heard nothing from outside. But in her mind's ear she could hear the sound of the word she had just spoken, its final syllable twanging like a tuning fork, infinitely receding to octaves above itself, infinitely returning. In what seemed scarcely a stride, she was in the next room, at the French window, brought there by that thin, directional vibration which not necessarily even the blind would hear. For she had recognized it. She had identified the accent of the scream.

The long window frame, its swollen wood shoved tight by her the night before, at first would not budge; then, as she put both hands on the hasp and braced her knees, it gave slowly, grinding inward, the heavy man-high bolt thumping down. Both sounds, too, fell into their proper places. That's what I heard before, she thought, the noise of a window opening or closing, exactly like mine. Two lines of them, down the six floors of the building, made twelve possibles. But that was of no importance now. Stepping up on the lintel, she spread the casements wide.

Yes, there was the bridge, one small arc of it, sheering off into the mist, beautiful against the night, as all bridges were. Now that she was outside, past all barriers, she could hear, with her ordinary ear, faint nickings that marred the silence, but these were only the surface scratches on a record that still revolved one low, continuous tone. No dogs do bark. That was the key to it, that her own hand, smoothing a remembered dog-collar, had been trying to give her. There were certain dog-whistles, to be bought anywhere—one had hung, with the unused leash, on a hook near a door in the country—which blew a summons so high above the human range that only a dog could hear it. What had summoned her last night would have been that much higher, audible only to those tuned in by necessity—the thin, soaring decibel of those who were no longer in the fold. Alone-oh. Alone-oh. That would have been the shape of it, of silence expelled from the mouth in one long relieving note, cool, irrepressible, the second one clapped short by the hand. No dog would have heard it. No animal but one was ever that alone.

She stepped out onto the fire escape. There must be legions of them, of us, she thought, in the dim alleyways, the high, flashing terraces—each one of them come to the end of his bookings, circling his small platform in space. And who would hear such a person? Not the log-girls, not for years and years. None of any age who, body to body, bed to bed, either in love or in the mutual pluck-pluck of hate—like the little girl and her mother—were still nested down. Reginald Warwick, stoppered in his special quiet, might hear it, turn to his Coco for confirmation which did not come, and persuade himself once again that it was only his affliction. Others lying awake snug as a bug, listening for that Old Nick, death, would hear the thin, sororal signal and not know what they had heard. But an endless assemblage of others all over the city would be waiting for it—all those sitting in the dark void of the one lamp quenched, the one syllable spoken —who would start up, some from sleep, to their windows . . . or were already there.

A car passed below. Instinctively, she flattened against the casement, but the car traveled on. Last night some-one, man or woman, would have been standing in one of the line of niches above and beneath hers—perhaps even a woman in a blue robe like her own. But literal distance or person would not matter; in that audience all would be the same. Looking up, she could see the tired, heated lavender of the mid-town sky, behind which lay that real imperial into which some men were already hurling their exquisitely signaling spheres. But this sound would come from breast to breast, at an altitude higher than any of those. She brought her fist to her mouth, in savage pride at having heard it, at belonging to a race some of whom could never adapt to any range less than that. *Some of us,* she thought, *are still responsible.*

Stepping forward, she leaned on the iron railing. At that moment, another car, traveling slowly by, hesitated opposite, its red dome light blinking. Mrs. Hazlitt stood very still. She watched until the police car went on again, inching ahead slowly, as if somebody inside were looking back. The two men inside there would never understand what she was waiting for. Hand clapped to her mouth, she herself had just understood. She was waiting for it— for its company. She was waiting for a second chance— to answer it. She was waiting for the scream to come again.

A CLEAN, WELL-LIGHTED PLACE

Ernest Hemingway

I T WAS LATE and every one had left the café except
an old man who sat in the shadow the leaves of the tree
made against the electric light. In the day time the street
was dusty, but at night the dew settled the dust and the
old man liked to sit late because he was deaf and now at
night it was quiet and he felt the difference. The two
waiters inside the café knew that the old man was a little
drunk, and while he was a good client they knew that if
he became too drunk he would leave without paying, so
they kept watch on him.

"Last week he tried to commit suicide," one waiter
said.

"Why?"

"He was in despair."

"What about?"

"Nothing."

"How do you know it was nothing?"

"He has plenty of money."

They sat together at a table that was close against the wall near the door of the café and looked at the terrace where the tables were all empty except where the old man sat in the shadow of the leaves of the tree that moved slightly in the wind. A girl and a soldier went by in the street. The streetlight shone on the brass number on his collar. The girl wore no head covering and hurried beside him.

"The guard will pick him up," one waiter said.

"What does it matter if he gets what he's after?"

"He had better get off the street now. The guard will get him. They went by five minutes ago."

The old man sitting in the shadow rapped on his saucer with his glass. The younger waiter went over to him.

"What do you want?"

The old man looked at him. "Another brandy," he said.

"You'll be drunk," the waiter said. The old man looked at him. The waiter went away.

"He'll stay all night," he said to his colleague. "I'm sleepy now. I never get into bed before three o'clock. He should have killed himself last week."

The waiter took the brandy bottle and another saucer

from the counter inside the café and marched out to the old man's table. He put down the saucer and poured the glass full of brandy.

"You should have killed yourself last week," he said to the deaf man. The old man motioned with his finger. "A little more," he said. The waiter poured on into the glass so that the brandy slopped over and ran down the stem into the top saucer of the pile. "Thank you," the old man said. The waiter took the bottle back inside the café. He sat down at the table with his colleague again.

"He's drunk now," he said.

"He's drunk every night."

"What did he want to kill himself for?"

"How should I know."

"How did he do it?"

"He hung himself with a rope."

"Who cut him down?"

"His niece."

"Why did they do it?"

"Fear for his soul."

"How much money has he got?"

"He's got plenty."

"He must be eighty years old."

"Anyway I should say he was eighty."

"I wish he would go home. I never get to bed before three o'clock. What kind of hour is that to go to bed?"

"He stays up because he likes it."

"He's lonely. I'm not lonely. I have a wife waiting in bed for me."

"He had a wife once too."

"A wife would be no good to him now."

"You can't tell. He might be better with a wife."

"His niece looks after him."

"I know. You said she cut him down."

"I wouldn't want to be that old. An old man is a nasty thing."

"Not always. This old man is clean. He drinks without spilling. Even now, drunk. Look at him."

"I don't want to look at him. I wish he would go home. He has no regard for those who must work."

The old man looked from his glass across the square, then over at the waiters.

"Another brandy," he said, pointing to his glass. The waiter who was in a hurry came over.

"Finished," he said, speaking with that omission of syntax stupid people employ when talking to drunken people or foreigners. "No more tonight. Close now."

"Another," said the old man.

"No. Finished." The waiter wiped the edge of the table with a towel and shook his head.

The old man stood up, slowly counted the saucers, took a leather coin purse from his pocket and paid for the drinks, leaving half a peseta tip.

The waiter watched him go down the street, a very old

man walking unsteadily but with dignity.

"Why didn't you let him stay and drink?" the unhurried waiter asked. They were putting up the shutters. "It is not half-past two."

"I want to go home to bed."

"What is an hour?"

"More to me than to him."

"An hour is the same."

"You talk like an old man yourself. He can buy a bottle and drink at home."

"It's not the same."

"No, it is not," agreed the waiter with a wife. He did not wish to be unjust. He was only in a hurry.

"And you? You have no fear of going home before your usual hour?"

"Are you trying to insult me?"

"No, hombre, only to make a joke."

"No," the waiter who was in a hurry said, rising from pulling down the metal shutters. "I have confidence. I am all confidence."

"You have youth, confidence, and a job," the older waiter said. "You have everything."

"And what do you lack?"

"Everything but work."

"You have everything I have."

"No. I have never had confidence and I am not young."

"Come on. Stop talking nonsense and lock up."

"I am of those who like to stay late at the café," the older waiter said. "With all those who do not want to go to bed. With all those who need a light for the night."

"I want to go home and into bed."

"We are of two different kinds," the older waiter said. He was now dressed to go home. "It is not only a question of youth and confidence although those things are very beautiful. Each night I am reluctant to close up because there may be some one who needs the café."

"Hombre, there are bodegas open all night long."

"You do not understand. This is a clean and pleasant café. It is well lighted. The light is very good and also, now, there are shadows of the leaves."

"Good night," said the younger waiter.

"Good night," the other said. Turning off the electric light he continued the conversation with himself. It is the light of course but it is necessary that the place be clean and pleasant. You do not want music. Certainly you do not want music. Nor can you stand before a bar with dignity although that is all that is provided for these hours. What did he fear? It was not fear or dread. It was a nothing that he knew too well. It was all a nothing and a man was nothing too. It was only that and light was all it needed and a certain cleanness and order. Some lived in it and never felt it but he knew it all was nada y pues nada y nada y pues nada. Our nada who art in nada, nada be thy name thy kingdom nada thy will be nada in nada as it is in nada. Give us this nada our daily nada and nada us our nada as we nada our nadas and nada us not into nada but deliver us from nada; pues nada. Hail nothing full of nothing, nothing is with thee. He smiled and stood before a bar with a shining steam pressure coffee machine.

"What's yours?" asked the barman.

"Nada."

"Otro loco mas," said the barman and turned away.

"A little cup," said the waiter.

The barman poured it for him.

"The light is very bright and pleasant but the bar is unpolished," the waiter said.

The barman looked at him but did not answer. It was too late at night for conversation.

"You want another copita?" the barman asked.

"No, thank you," said the waiter and went out. He disliked bars and bodegas. A clean, well-lighted café was a very different thing. Now, without thinking further, he would go home to his room. He would lie in the bed and finally, with daylight, he would go to sleep. After all, he said to himself, it is probably only insomnia. Many must have it.

A FORGOTTEN POET

Vladimir Nabokov

I N 1899, IN THE ponderous, comfortable padded St.
Petersburg of those days, a prominent cultural organi-
zation, the Society for the Advancement of Russian Literature, decided to honor in a grand way the memory of
the poet Konstantin Perov, who had died half a century
before at the ardent age of four-and-twenty. He had been
styled the Russian Rimbaud and, although the French
boy surpassed him in genius, such a comparison is not
wholly unjustified. When only eighteen he composed his
remarkable *Georgian Nights,* a long, rambling "dream
epic," certain passages of which rip the veil of its traditional Oriental setting to produce that heavenly draft
which suddenly locates the sensorial effect of true poetry
right between one's shoulder blades.

This was followed three years later by a volume of poems: he had got hold of some German philosopher or other, and several of these pieces are distressing because of the grotesque attempt at combining an authentic lyrical spasm with a metaphysical explanation of the universe; but the rest are still as vivid and unusual as they were in the days when that queer youth dislocated the Russian vocabulary and twisted the necks of accepted epithets in order to make poetry splutter and scream instead of twittering. Most readers like best those poems of his where the ideas of emancipation, so characteristic of the Russian fifties, are expressed in a glorious storm of obscure eloquence, which, as one critic put it, "does not show you the enemy but makes you fairly burst with the longing to fight." Personally I prefer the purer and at the same time bumpier lyrics such as "The Gypsy" or "The Bat."

Perov was the son of a small landowner of whom the only thing known is that he tried planting tea on his estate near Luga. Young Konstantin (to use a biographical intonation) spent most of his time in St. Petersburg vaguely attending the University, then vaguely looking for a clerical job—little indeed is known of his activities beyond such trivialities as can be deduced from the general trends of his set. A passage in the correspondence of the famous poet Nekrasov, who happened to meet him once in a bookshop, conveys the image of a sulky, unbalanced, "clumsy and fierce" young man with "the eyes of a child and the shoulders of a furniture mover."

He is also mentioned in a police report as "conversing in low tones with two other students" in a coffeehouse on Nevsky Avenue. And his sister, who married a merchant from Riga, is said to have deplored the poet's emotional adventures with seamstresses and washerwomen. In the autumn of 1849 he visited his father with the special intent of obtaining money for a trip to Spain. His father, a man of simple reactions, slapped him on the face; and a few days later the poor boy was drowned while bathing in the neighboring river. His clothes and a half-eaten apple were found lying under a birch tree, but the body was never recovered.

His fame was sluggish: a passage from the *Georgian Nights,* always the same one, in all anthologies; a violent article by the radical critic Dobrolubov, in 1859, lauding the revolutionary innuendoes of his weakest poems; a general notion in the eighties that a reactionary atmosphere had thwarted and finally destroyed a fine if somewhat inarticulate talent—this was about all.

In the nineties, because of a healthier interest in poetry, coinciding as it sometimes does with a sturdy and dull political era, a flurry of rediscovery started around Perov's rhymes while, on the other hand, the liberal-minded were not averse to following Dobrolubov's cue. The subscription for a monument in one of the public parks proved a perfect success. A leading publisher collected all the scraps of information available in regard to Perov's life and issued his complete works in one fairly plump volume. The monthlies contributed several scholarly surveys. The commemorative meeting in one of the best halls of the capital attracted a crowd.

II

A few minutes before the start, while the speakers were still assembled in a committee room behind the stage, the door opened gustily and there entered a sturdy old man, clad in a frock coat that had seen—on his or on somebody else's shoulders—better times. Without paying the slightest heed to the admonishments of a couple of ribbon-badged University students who, in their capacity of attendants, were attempting to restrain him, he proceeded with perfect dignity towards the committee, bowed, and said, "I am Perov."

A friend of mine, almost twice my age and now the only surviving witness of the event, tells me that the chairman (who as a newspaper editor had a great deal of experience in the matter of extravagant intruders) said without even looking up, "Kick him out." Nobody did —perhaps because one is apt to show a certain courtesy to an old gentleman who is supposedly very drunk. He sat down at the table and, selecting the mildest-looking person, Slavsky, a translator of Longfellow, Heine, and Sully-Prudhomme (and later a member of the terrorist group), asked in a matter-of-fact tone whether the "monument money" had already been collected, and if so, when could he have it.

All the accounts agree on the singularly quiet way in which he made his claim. He did not press his point. He merely stated it as if absolutely unconscious of any possibility of his being disbelieved. What impressed one was that at the very beginning of that weird affair, in that secluded room, among those distinguished men, there he was with his patriarchal beard, faded brown eyes, and potato nose, sedately inquiring about the benefits from the proceedings without even bothering to produce such proofs as might have been faked by an ordinary impostor.

"Are you a relative?" asked someone.

"My name is Konstantin Konstantinovich Perov," said the old man patiently. "I am given to understand that a descendant of my family is in the hall, but that is neither here nor there."

"How old are you?" asked Slavsky.

"I am seventy-four," he replied, "and the victim of several poor crops in succession."

"You are surely aware," remarked the actor Yermakov, "that the poet whose memory we are celebrating tonight was drowned in the river Oredezh exactly fifty years ago."

"*Vzdor*—nonsense," retorted the old man. "I staged that business for reasons of my own."

"And now, my dear fellow," said the chairman, "I really think you must go."

They dismissed him from their consciousness and flocked out onto the severely lighted platform where another committee table, draped in solemn red cloth, with the necessary number of chairs behind it, had been hypnotizing the audience for some time with the glint of its traditional decanter. To the left of this, one could admire the oil painting loaned by the Sheremetevski Art Gallery: it represented Perov at twenty-two, a swarthy young man with romantic hair and an open shirt collar. The picture stand was piously camouflaged by means of leaves and flowers. A lectern with another decanter loomed in front and a grand piano was waiting in the wings to be rolled in later for the musical part of the program.

The hall was well packed with literary people, enlightened lawyers, schoolteachers, scholars, eager university students of both sexes, and the like. A few humble agents of the secret police had been delegated to attend the meeting in inconspicuous spots of the hall, as the government knew by experience that the most staid cultural assemblies had a queer knack of slipping into an orgy of revolutionary propaganda. The fact that one of Perov's first poems contained a veiled but benevolent allusion to the insurrection of 1825 suggested taking certain precautions: one never could tell what might happen after a public mouthing of such lines as "the gloomy sough of Siberian larches communicates with the underground ore—*sibirskikh pikht oogrewmyi shorokh s podzemnoy snositsa roodoy.*"

As one of the accounts has it, "soon one became aware that something vaguely resembling a Dostoyevskian row [the author is thinking of a famous slapstick chapter in *The Possessed*] was creating an atmosphere of awkwardness and suspense." This was due to the fact that the old gentleman deliberately followed the seven members of the jubilee committee onto the platform and then attempted to sit down with them at the table. The chairman, being mainly intent upon avoiding a scuffle in full view of the audience, did his best to make him desist. Under the public disguise of a polite smile he whispered to the patriarch that he would have him ejected from the hall if he did not let go the back of the chair which Slavsky, with a nonchalant air but with a grip of iron, was covertly wresting from under the old man's gnarled hand. The old man refused but lost his hold and was left without a seat. He glanced around, noticed the piano stool in the wings and coolly pulled it onto the stage just a fraction of a second before the hands of a screened attendant tried to snatch it back. He seated himself at some distance from the table and immediately became exhibit number one.

Here the committee made the fatal mistake of again dismissing his presence from their minds: they were, let it be repeated, particularly anxious to avoid a scene; and moreover, the blue hydrangea next to the picture stand half concealed the obnoxious party from their physical vision. Unfortunately, the old gentleman was most conspicuous to the audience, as he sat there on his unseemly pedestal (with its rotatory potentialities hinted at by a recurrent creaking), opening his spectacle case and breathing fishlike upon his glasses, perfectly calm and comfortable, his venerable head, shabby black clothes, and elastic-sided boots simultaneously suggesting the needy Russian professor and the prosperous Russian undertaker.

The chairman went up to the lectern and launched upon his introductory speech. Whisperings rippled all over the audience, for people were naturally curious to know who the old fellow was. Firmly bespectacled, with his hands on his knees, he peered sideways at the portrait, then turned away from it and inspected the front row. Answering glances could not help shuttling between the shiny dome of his head and the curly head of the portrait, for during the chairman's long speech the details of the intrusion spread, and the imagination of some started to toy with the idea that a poet belonging to an almost legendary period, snugly relegated to it by textbooks, an anachronistic creature, a live fossil in the nets of an ignorant fisherman, a kind of Rip van Winkle, was actually attending in his drab dotage the reunion dedicated to the glory of his youth.

". . . let the name of Perov," said the chairman, ending his speech, "be never. forgotten by thinking Russia. Tyutchev has said that Pushkin will always be remembered by our country as a first love. In regard to Perov we may say that he was Russia's first experience in freedom. To a superficial observer this freedom may seem limited to Perov's phenomenal lavishness of poetical images which appeal more to the artist than to the citizen. But we, representatives of a more sober generation, are inclined to decipher for ourselves a deeper, more vital, more human, and more social sense in such lines of his as

"When the last snow hides in the shade of the cemetery wall
and the coat of my neighbor's black horse
shows a swift blue sheen in the swift April sun,
and the puddles are as many heavens cupped
     in the Negro-hands of the Earth,
then my heart goes out in its tattered cloak
to visit the poor, the blind, the foolish,
the round backs slaving for the round bellies,
all those whose eyes dulled by care or lust do not see
the holes in the snow, the blue horse, the miraculous
     puddle."

A burst of applause greeted this, but all of a sudden there was a break in the clapping, and then disharmonious gusts of laughter; for, as the chairman, still vibrating with the words he had just uttered, went back to the table, the bearded stranger got up and acknowledged the applause by means of jerky nods and awkward wavings of the hand, his expression combining formal gratitude with a certain impatience. Slavsky and a couple of attendants made a desperate attempt to bundle him away, but from the depth of the audience there arose the cries of "Shame, shame!" and *"Astavte starika*—Leave the old man alone!"

I find in one of the accounts the suggestion that there were accomplices among the audience, but I think that mass compassion, which may come as unexpectedly as mass vindictiveness, is sufficient to explain the turn things were taking. In spite of having to cope with three men the *"starik"* managed to retain a remarkable dignity of demeanor, and when his halfhearted assailants retired and he retrieved the piano stool that had been knocked down during the struggle, there was a murmur of satisfaction. However, the regrettable fact remained that the atmosphere of the meeting was hopelessly impaired. The younger and rowdier members of the audience were beginning to enjoy themselves hugely. The chairman, his nostrils quivering, poured himself out a tumbler of water. Two secret agents were cautiously exchanging glances from two different points of the house.

III

The speech of the chairman was followed by the treasurer's account of the sums received from various institutions and private persons for the erection of a Perov monument in one of the suburban parks. The old man unhurriedly produced a bit of paper and a stubby pencil and, propping the paper on his knee, began to check the figures which were being mentioned. Then the granddaughter of Perov's sister appeared for a moment on the stage. The organizers had had some trouble with this item of the program since the person in question, a fat, popeyed, wax-pale young woman, was being treated for melancholia in a home for mental patients. With twisted mouth and all dressed up in pathetic pink, she was shown to the audience for a moment and then whisked back into the firm hands of a buxom woman delegated by the home.

When Yermakov, who in those days was the darling of theatergoers, a kind of "beau ténor" in terms of the drama, began delivering in his chocolate-cream voice the Prince's speech from the *Georgian Nights,* it became clear that even his best fans were more interested in the reactions of the old man than in the beauty of the delivery. At the lines

> *If metal is immortal, then somewhere*
> *there lies the burnished button that I lost*

upon my seventh birthday in a garden.
Find me that button and my soul will know
that every soul is saved and stored and treasured

a chink appeared for the first time in his composure and he slowly unfolded a large handkerchief and lustily blew his nose—a sound which sent Yermakov's heavily adumbrated, diamond-bright eye squinting like that of a timorous steed.

The handkerchief was returned to the folds of the coat and only several seconds *after* this did it become noticeable to the people in the first row that tears were trickling from under his glasses. He did not attempt to wipe them, though once or twice his hand did go up to his spectacles with claw-wise spread fingers, but it dropped again, as if by any such gesture (and this was the culminating point of the whole delicate masterpiece) he was afraid to attract attention to his tears. The tremendous applause that followed the recitation was certainly more a tribute to the old man's performance than to the poem in Yermakov's rendering. Then, as soon as the applause petered out, he stood up and marched towards the edge of the platform.

There was no attempt on the part of the committee to stop him, and this for two reasons. First, the chairman, driven to exasperation by the old man's conspicuous behavior, had gone out for a moment and given a certain

order. In the second place, a medley of strange doubts
was beginning to unnerve some of the organizers, so that
there was a complete hush when the old man placed his
elbows on the reading stand.

"And this is fame," he said in such a husky voice that
from the back rows there came cries of *"Gromche, gromche
—Louder, louder!"*

"I am saying that this is fame," he repeated, grimly
peering over his spectacles at the audience. "A score of
frivolous poems, words made to joggle and jingle, and
a man's name is remembered as if he had been of some
use to humanity! No, gentlemen, do not delude your-
selves. Our empire and the throne of our father the Tsar
still stand as they stood, akin to frozen thunder in their
invulnerable might, and the misguided youth who scribbled rebellious verse half a century ago is now a law-
abiding old man respected by honest citizens. An old
man, let me add, who needs your protection. I am the
victim of the elements: the land I had plowed with my
sweat, the lambs I had personally suckled, the wheat I
had seen waving its golden arms—"

It was then that two enormous policemen quickly and
painlessly removed the old man. The audience had a
glimpse of his being rushed out—his dickey protruding
one way, his beard the other, a cuff dangling from his
wrist, but still that gravity and that pride in his eyes.

When reporting the celebration, the leading dailies

referred only in passing to the "regrettable incident" that had marred it. But the disreputable *St. Petersburg Record,* a lurid and reactionary rag edited by the brothers Kherstov for the benefit of the lower middle class and of a blissfully semiliterate substratum of working people, blazed forth with a series of articles maintaining that the "regrettable incident" was nothing less than the reappearance of the authentic Perov.

IV

In the meantime, the old man had been collected by the very wealthy and vulgarly eccentric merchant Gromov, whose household was full of vagabond monks, quack doctors, and "pogromystics." The *Record* printed interviews with the impostor. In these the latter said dreadful things about the "lackeys of the revolutionary party" who had cheated him of his identity and robbed him of his money. This money he proposed to obtain by law from the publishers of Perov's complete works. A drunken scholar attached to the Gromov household pointed out the (unfortunately rather striking) similarity between the old man's features and those of the portrait.

There appeared a detailed but most implausible account of his having staged a suicide in order to lead a Christian life in the bosom of Saint Russia. He had been everything: a peddler, a bird catcher, a ferryman on the

Volga, and had wound up by acquiring a bit of land in a remote province. I have seen a copy of a sordid-looking booklet, *The Death and Resurrection of Konstantin Perov*, which used to be sold on the streets by shivering beggars, together with the *Adventures of the Marquis de Sade* and the *Memoirs of an Amazon*.

My best find, however, in looking through old files, is a smudgy photograph of the bearded impostor perched upon the marble of the unfinished Perov monument in a leafless park. He is seen standing very straight with his arms folded; he wears a round fur cap and a new pair of galoshes but no overcoat; a little crowd of his backers is gathered at his feet, and their little white faces stare into the camera with that special navel-eyed, self-complacent expression peculiar to old pictures of lynching parties.

Given this atmosphere of florid hooliganism and reactionary smugness (so closely linked up with governmental ideas in Russia, no matter whether the Tsar be called Alexander, Nicholas, or Joe), the intelligentsia could hardly bear to visualize the disaster of identifying the pure, ardent, revolutionary-minded Perov as represented by his poems with a vulgar old man wallowing in a painted pigsty. The tragic part was that while neither Gromov nor the Kherstov brothers really believed the purveyor of their fun was the true Perov, many honest, cultivated people had become obsessed by the impossible thought that what they had ejected was Truth and Justice.

As a recently published letter from Slavsky to Korolenko has it: "One shudders to think that a gift of destiny
unparalleled in history, the Lazaruslike resurrection of a
great poet of the past, may be ungratefully ignored—nay,
even more, deemed a fiendish deceit on the part of a man
whose only crime has been half a century of silence and
a few minutes of wild talk." The wording is muddled but
the gist is clear: intellectual Russia was less afraid of
falling victim to a hoax than of sponsoring a hideous
blunder. But there was something she was still more
afraid of, and that was the destruction of an ideal; for
your radical is ready to upset everything in the world
except any such trivial bauble, no matter how doubtful
and dusty, that for some reason radicalism has enshrined.

It is rumored that at a certain secret session of the
Society for the Advancement of Russian Literature the
numerous insulting epistles that the old man kept sending in were carefully compared by experts with a very old
letter written by the poet in his teens. It had been discovered in a certain private archive, was believed to be the
only sample of Perov's hand, and none except the scholars who pored over its faded ink knew of its existence.
Neither do we know what their findings were.

It is further rumored that a lump of money was
amassed and that the old man was approached without
the knowledge of his disgraceful companions. Apparently, a substantial monthly pension was to be granted

him under the condition that he return at once to his farm and stay there in decorous silence and oblivion. Apparently, too, the offer was accepted, for he vanished as jerkily as he had appeared, while Gromov consoled himself for the loss of his pet by adopting a shady hypnotizer of French extraction who a year or two later was to enjoy some success at the Court.

The monument was duly unveiled and became a great favorite with the local pigeons. The sales of the collected works fizzled out genteelly in the middle of a fourth edition. Finally, a few years later, in the region where Perov had been born, the oldest though not necessarily the brightest inhabitant told a lady journalist that he remembered his father telling him of finding a skeleton in a reedy part of the river.

V

This would have been all had not the revolution come, turning up slabs of rich earth together with the white rootlets of little plants and fat mauve worms which otherwise would have remained buried. When, in the early twenties, in the dark, hungry, but morbidly active city, various odd cultural institutions sprouted (such as bookshops where famous but destitute writers sold their own books, and so on), somebody or other earned a couple of months' living by arranging a little Perov museum, and this led to yet another resurrection.

The exhibits? All of them except one (the letter). A second-hand past in a shabby hall. The oval-shaped eyes and brown locks of the precious Sheremetevsky portrait (with a crack in the region of the open collar suggesting a tentative beheading); a battered volume of the *Georgian Nights* that was thought to have belonged to Nekrasov; an indifferent photograph of the village school built on the spot where the poet's father had owned a house and an orchard. An old glove that some visitor to the museum had forgotten. Several editions of Perov's works distributed in such a way as to occupy the greatest possible space.

And because all these poor relics still refused to form a happy family, several period articles had been added, such as the dressing gown that a famous radical critic had worn in his rococo study, and the chains he had worn in his wooden Siberian prison. But there again, since neither this nor the portraits of various writers of the time were bulky enough, a model of the first railway train to run in Russia (in the forties, between St. Petersburg and Tsarskoyeselo) had been installed in the middle of that dismal room.

The old man, now well over ninety but still articulate in speech and reasonably erect in carriage, would show you around the place as if he were your host instead of being the janitor. One had the odd impression that presently he would lead you into the next (non-existing) room, where supper would be served. All that he really possessed, however, was a stove behind a screen and the bench on which he slept; but if you bought one of the books exhibited for sale at the entrance he would autograph it for you as a matter of course.

Then one morning he was found dead on his bench by the woman who brought him his food. Three quarrelsome families lived for a while in the museum, and soon nothing remained of its contents. And as if some great hand with a great rasping sound had torn out a great bunch of pages from a number of books, or as if some frivolous story writer had bottled an imp of fiction in the vessel of truth, or as if. . . .

But no matter. Somehow or other, in the next twenty years or so, Russia lost all contact with Perov's poetry. Young Soviet citizens know as little about his works as they do about mine. No doubt a time will come when he will be republished and readmired; still, one cannot help feeling that, as things stand, people are missing a great deal. One wonders also what future historians will make of the old man and his extraordinary contention. But that, of course, is a matter of secondary importance.

TOMORROW AND TOMORROW AND TOMORROW

Kurt Vonnegut, Jr.

THE YEAR WAS 2158 A.D., and Lou and Emerald Schwartz were whispering on the balcony outside Lou's family's apartment on the seventy-sixth floor of Building 257 in Alden Village, a New York housing development that covered what had once been known as Southern Connecticut. When Lou and Emerald had married, Em's parents had tearfully described the marriage as being between May and December; but now, with Lou one hundred and twelve and Em ninety-three, Em's parents had to admit that the match had worked out well.

But Em and Lou weren't without their troubles, and they were out in the nippy air of the balcony because of them.

"Sometimes I get so mad, I feel like just up and diluting his anti-gerasone," said Em.

"That'd be against Nature, Em," said Lou, "it'd be murder. Besides, if he caught us tinkering with his anti-gerasone, not only would he disinherit us, he'd bust my neck. Just because he's one hundred and seventy-two doesn't mean Gramps isn't strong as a bull."

"Against Nature," said Em. "Who knows what Nature's like anymore? Ohhhhh—I don't guess I could ever bring myself to dilute his anti-gerasone or anything like that, but, gosh, Lou, a body can't help thinking Gramps is never going to leave if somebody doesn't help him along a little. Golly—we're so crowded a person can hardly turn around, and Verna's dying for a baby, and Melissa's gone thirty years without one." She stamped her feet. "I get so sick of seeing his wrinkled old face, watching him take the only private room and the best chair and the best food, and getting to pick out what to watch on TV, and running everybody's life by changing his will all the time."

"Well, after all," said Lou bleakly, "Gramps *is* head of the family. And he can't help being wrinkled like he is. He was seventy before anti-gerasone was invented. He's going to leave, Em. Just give him time. It's his business. I know he's tough to live with, but be patient. It wouldn't do to do anything that'd rile him. After all, we've got it better'n anybody else, there on the daybed."

"How much longer do you think we'll get to sleep on

the daybed before he picks another pet? The world's record's two months, isn't it?"

"Mom and Pop had it that long once, I guess."

"When *is* he going to leave, Lou?" said Emerald.

"Well, he's talking about giving up anti-gerasone right after the Five-Hundred-Mile Speedway Race."

"Yes—and before that it was the Olympics, and before that the World's Series, and before that the Presidential Elections, and before that I-don't-know-what. It's been just one excuse after another for fifty years now. I don't think we're ever going to get a room to ourselves or an egg or anything."

"All right—call me a failure!" said Lou. "What can I do? I work hard and make good money, but the whole thing, practically, is taxed away for defense and old age pensions. And if it wasn't taxed away, where you think we'd find a vacant room to rent? Iowa, maybe? Well, who wants to live on the outskirts of Chicago?"

Em put her arms around his neck. "Lou, hon, I'm not calling you a failure. The Lord knows you're not. You just haven't had a chance to be anything or have anything because Gramps and the rest of his generation won't leave and let somebody else take over."

"Yeah, yeah," said Lou gloomily. "You can't exactly blame 'em, though, can you? I mean, I wonder how quick we'll knock off the anti-gerasone when we get Gramps' age."

"Sometimes I wish there wasn't any such thing as anti-gerasone!" said Emerald passionately. "Or I wish it was made out of something real expensive and hard-to-get instead of mud and dandelions. Sometimes I wish folks just up and died regular as clockwork, without anything to say about it, instead of deciding themselves how long they're going to stay around. There ought to be a law against selling the stuff to anybody over one hundred and fifty."

"Fat chance of that," said Lou, "with all the money and votes the old people've got." He looked at her closely. "You ready to up and die, Em?"

"Well, for heaven's sakes, what a thing to say to your wife. Hon! I'm not even one hundred yet." She ran her hands lightly over her firm, youthful figure, as though for confirmation. "The best years of my life are still ahead of me. But you can bet that when one hundred and fifty rolls around, old Em's going to pour her anti-gerasone down the sink, and quit taking up room, and she'll do it smiling."

"Sure, sure," said Lou, "you bet. That's what they all say. How many you heard of doing it?"

"There was that man in Delaware."

"Aren't you getting kind of tired of talking about him, Em? That was five months ago."

"All right, then—Gramma Winkler, right here in the same building."

"She got smeared by a subway."

"That's just the way she picked to go," said Em.

"Then what was she doing carrying a six-pack of anti-gerasone when she got it?"

Emerald shook her head wearily and covered her eyes. "I dunno, I dunno, I dunno. All I know is, something's just got to be done." She sighed. "Sometimes I wish they'd left a couple of diseases kicking around somewhere, so I could get one and go to bed for a little while. Too many people!" she cried, and her words cackled and gabbled and died in a thousand asphalt-paved, skyscraper-walled courtyards.

Lou laid his hand on her shoulder tenderly. "Aw, hon, I hate to see you down in the dumps like this."

"If we just had a car, like the folks used to in the old days," said Em, "we could go for a drive, and get away from people for a little while. Gee—if *those* weren't the days!"

"Yeah," said Lou, "before they'd used up all the metal."

"We'd hop in, and Pop'd drive up to a filling station and say, 'Fillerup!' "

"That *was* the nuts, wasn't it—before they'd used up all the gasoline."

"And we'd go for a carefree ride in the country."

"Yeah—all seems like a fairyland now, doesn't it, Em? Hard to believe there really used to be all that space between cities."

"And when we got hungry," said Em, "we'd find ourselves a restaurant, and walk in, big as you please and say,
'I'll have a steak and French-fries, I believe,' or, 'How
are the pork chops today?' " She licked her lips, and her
eyes glistened.

"Yeah man!" growled Lou. "How'd you like a ham-
burger with the works, Em?"

"Mmmmmmmm."

"If anybody'd offered us processed seaweed in those
days, we would have spit right in his eye, huh, Em?"

"Or processed sawdust," said Em.

Doggedly, Lou tried to find the cheery side of the
situation. "Well, anyway, they've got the stuff so it tastes
a lot less like seaweed and sawdust than it did at first; and
they say it's actually better for us than what we used to
eat."

"I felt fine!" said Em fiercely.

Lou shrugged. "Well, you've got to realize, the
world wouldn't be able to support twelve billion people if it wasn't for processed seaweed and sawdust. I
mean, it's a wonderful thing, really. I guess. That's
what they say."

"They say the first thing that pops into their heads,"
said Em. She closed her eyes. "Golly—remember shopping, Lou? Remember how the stores used to fight to get
our folks to buy something? You didn't have to wait for
somebody to die to get a bed or chairs or a stove or
anything like that. Just went in—bing!—and bought

whatever you wanted. Gee whiz that was nice, before they used up all the raw materials. I was just a little kid then, but I can remember so plain."

Depressed, Lou walked listlessly to the balcony's edge, and looked up at the clean, cold, bright stars against the black velvet of infinity. "Remember when we used to be bugs on science fiction, Em? Flight seventeen, leaving for Mars, launching ramp twelve. 'Board! All non-technical personnel kindly remain in bunkers. Ten seconds . . . nine . . . eight . . . seven . . . six . . . five . . . four . . . three . . . two . . . *one! Main Stage! Barrrrrroooom!*"

"Why worry about what was going on on Earth?" said Em, looking up at the stars with him. "In another few years, we'd all be shooting through space to start life all over again on a new planet."

Lou sighed. "Only it turns out you need something about twice the size of the Empire State Building to get one lousy colonist to Mars. And for another couple of trillion bucks he could take his wife and dog. *That's* the way to lick overpopulation—*emigrate!*"

"Lou—?"

"Hmmm?"

"When's the Five-Hundred-Mile Speedway Race?"

"Uh—Memorial Day, May thirtieth."

She bit her lip. "Was that awful of me to ask?"

"Not very, I guess. Everybody in the apartment's looked it up to make sure."

"I don't want to be awful," said Em, "but you've just

got to talk over these things now and then, and get them out of your system."

"Sure you do. Feel better?"

"Yes—and I'm not going to lose my temper anymore, and I'm going to be just as nice to him as I know how."

"That's my Em."

They squared their shoulders, smiled bravely, and went back inside.

Gramps Schwartz, his chin resting on his hands, his hands on the crook of his cane, was staring irascibly at the five-foot television screen that dominated the room. On the screen, a news commentator was summarizing the day's happenings. Every thirty seconds or so, Gramps would jab the floor with his cane-tip and shout, "Hell! We did that a hundred years ago!"

Emerald and Lou, coming in from the balcony, were obliged to take seats in the back row, behind Lou's father and mother, brother and sister-in-law, son and daughter-in-law, grandson and wife, granddaughter and husband, great-grandson and wife, nephew and wife, grandnephew and wife, great-grandniece and husband, great-grandnephew and wife, and, of course, Gramps, who was in front of everybody. All, save Gramps, who was somewhat withered and bent, seemed, by pre-anti-gerasone standards, to be about the same age—to be somewhere in their late twenties or early thirties.

"Meanwhile," the commentator was saying, *"Council Bluffs, Iowa, was still threatened by stark tragedy. But two hundred weary rescue workers have refused to give up hope, and continue to dig in an effort to save Elbert Haggedorn, one hundred and eighty-three, who has been wedged for two days in a . . ."*

"I wish he'd get something more cheerful," Emerald whispered to Lou.

"Silence!" cried Gramps. "Next one shoots off his big bazoo while the TV's on is gonna find hisself cut off without a dollar—" and here his voice suddenly softened and sweetened—"when they wave that checkered flag at the Indianapolis Speedway, and old Gramps gets ready for the Big Trip Up Yonder." He sniffed sentimentally, while his heirs concentrated desperately on not making the slightest sound. For them, the poignancy of the prospective Big Trip had been dulled somewhat by its having been mentioned by Gramps about once a day for fifty years.

"Dr. Brainard Keyes Bullard," said the commentator, *"President of Wyandotte College, said in an address tonight that most of the world's ills can be traced to the fact that Man's knowledge of himself has not kept pace with his knowledge of the physical world."*

"Hell!" said Gramps. "We said that a hundred years ago!"

"In Chicago tonight," said the commentator, *"a special*

celebration is taking place in the Chicago Lying-in Hospital. The guest of honor is Lowell W. Hitz, age zero. Hitz, born this morning, is the twenty-five-millionth child to be born in the hospital." The commentator faded, and was replaced on the screen by young Hitz, who squalled furiously.

"Hell," whispered Lou to Emerald, "we said that a hundred years ago."

"I heard that!" shouted Gramps. He snapped off the television set, and his petrified descendants stared silently at the screen. "You, there, boy—"

"I didn't mean anything by it, sir," said Lou.

"Get me my will. You know where it is. You kids *all* know where it is. Fetch, boy!"

Lou nodded dully, and found himself going down the hall, picking his way over bedding to Gramps' room, the only private room in the Schwartz apartment. The other rooms were the bathroom, the living room, and the wide, windowless hallway, which was originally intended to serve as a dining area, and which had a kitchenette in one end. Six mattresses and four sleeping bags were dispersed in the hallway and living room, and the day-bed, in the living room, accommodated the eleventh couple, the favorites of the moment.

On Gramps' bureau was his will, smeared, dog-eared, perforated, and blotched with hundreds of additions, deletions, accusations, conditions, warnings, advice, and homely philosophy. The document was, Lou reflected, a fifty-year diary, all jammed onto two sheets—a garbled, illegible log of day after day of strife. This day, Lou would be disinherited for the eleventh time, and it would take him perhaps six months of impeccable behavior to regain the promise of a share in the estate.

"Boy!" called Gramps.

"Coming, sir." Lou hurried back into the living room, and handed Gramps the will.

"Pen!" said Gramps.

He was instantly offered eleven pens, one from each couple.

"Not *that* leaky thing," he said, brushing Lou's pen aside. "Ah, there's a nice one. Good boy, Willy." He accepted Willy's pen. That was the tip they'd all been waiting for. Willy, then, Lou's father, was the new favorite.

Willy, who looked almost as young as Lou, though one hundred and forty-two, did a poor job of concealing his pleasure. He glanced shyly at the daybed, which would become his, and from which Lou and Emerald would have to move back into the hall, back to the worst spot of all by the bathroom door.

Gramps missed none of the high drama he'd authored, and he gave his own familiar role everything he had. Frowning and running his finger along each line, as though he were seeing the will for the first time, he read aloud in a deep, portentous monotone, like a bass tone on a cathedral organ:

"I, Harold D. Schwartz, residing in Building 257 of

Alden Village, New York City, do hereby make, publish, and declare this to be my last Will and Testament, hereby revoking any and all former wills and codicils by me at any time heretofore made." He blew his nose importantly, and went on, not missing a word, and repeating many for emphasis—repeating in particular his ever-more-elaborate specifications for a funeral.

At the end of these specifications, Gramps was so choked with emotion that Lou thought he might forget why he'd gotten out the will in the first place. But Gramps heroically brought his powerful emotions under control, and, after erasing for a full minute, he began to write and speak at the same time. Lou could have spoken his lines for him, he'd heard them so often.

"I have had many heartbreaks ere leaving this vale of tears for a better land," Gramps said and wrote. "But the deepest hurt of all has been dealt me by—" He looked around the group, trying to remember who the malefactor was.

Everyone looked helpfully at Lou, who held up his hand resignedly.

Gramps nodded, remembering, and completed the sentence: "my great-grandson, Louis J. Schwartz."

"Grandson, sir," said Lou.

"Don't quibble. You're in deep enough now, young man," said Gramps, but he changed the trifle. And from there he went without a misstep through the phrasing of

the disinheritance, causes for which were disrespectful-
ness and quibbling.

In the paragraph following, the paragraph that had
belonged to everyone in the room at one time or another, Lou's name was scratched out and Willy's substituted as heir to the apartment and, the biggest plum of
all, the double bed in the private bedroom. "So!" said
Gramps, beaming. He erased the date at the foot of the
will, and substituted a new one, including the time of
day. "Well—time to watch the McGarvey Family." The
McGarvey Family was a television serial that Gramps had
been following since he was sixty, or for one hundred
and twelve years. "I can't wait to see what's going to
happen next," he said.

Lou detached himself from the group and lay down on
his bed of pain by the bathroom door. He wished Em
would join him, and he wondered where she was.

He dozed for a few moments, until he was disturbed
by someone's stepping over him to get into the bathroom. A moment later, he heard a faint gurgling sound,
as though something were being poured down the washbasin drain. Suddenly, it entered his mind that Em had
cracked up, and that she was in there doing something
drastic about Gramps.

"Em—?" he whispered through the panel. There was
no reply, and Lou pressed against the door. The worn
lock, whose bolt barely engaged its socket, held for a

second, then let the door swing inward.

"Morty!" gasped Lou.

Lou's great-grandnephew, Mortimer, who had just married and brought his wife home to the Schwartz menage, looked at Lou with consternation and surprise. Morty kicked the door shut, but not before Lou had glimpsed what was in his hand—Gramps' enormous economy-size bottle of anti-gerasone, which had been half-emptied, and which Morty was refilling to the top with tap water.

A moment later, Morty came out, glared defiantly at Lou, and brushed past him wordlessly to rejoin his pretty bride.

Shocked, Lou didn't know what on earth to do. He couldn't let Gramps take the mousetrapped anti-gerasone; but if he warned Gramps about it, Gramps would certainly make life in the apartment, which was merely insufferable now, harrowing.

Lou glanced into the living room, and saw that the Schwartzes, Emerald among them, were momentarily at rest, relishing the botches that McGarveys had made of *their* lives. Stealthily, he went into the bathroom, locked the door as well as he could, and began to pour the contents of Gramps' bottle down the drain. He was going to refill it with full-strength anti-gerasone from the twenty-two smaller bottles on the shelf. The bottle contained a half-gallon, and its neck was small, so it seemed to Lou that the emptying would take forever. And the almost imperceptible smell of anti-gerasone, like Worcestershire sauce, now seemed to Lou, in his nervousness, to be pouring out into the rest of the apartment through the keyhole and under the door.

"Gloog-gloog-gloog-gloog-," went the bottle monotonously. Suddenly, up came the sound of music from the living room, and there were murmurs and the scraping of chair legs on the floor. *"Thus ends,"* said the television announcer, *"the 29,121st chapter in the life of your neighbors and mine, the McGarveys."* Footsteps were coming down the hall. There was a knock on the bathroom door.

"Just a sec," called Lou cheerily. Desperately, he shook the big bottle, trying to speed up the flow. His palms slipped on the wet glass, and the heavy bottle smashed to splinters on the tile floor.

The door sprung open, and Gramps, dumfounded, stared at the mess.

Lou grinned engagingly through his nausea, and, for want of anything remotely resembling a thought, he waited for Gramps to speak.

"Well, boy," said Gramps at last, "looks like you've got a little tidying up to do."

And that was all he said. He turned around, elbowed his way through the crowd, and locked himself in his bedroom.

The Schwartzes contemplated Lou in incredulous silence for a moment longer, and then hurried back to the living room, as though some of his horrible guilt would taint them, too, if they looked too long. Morty stayed behind long enough to give Lou a quizzical, annoyed glance. Then he, too, went into the living room, leaving only Emerald standing in the doorway.

Tears streamed over her cheeks. "Oh, you poor lamb —please don't look so awful. It was my fault. I put you up to this."

"No," said Lou, finding his voice, "really you didn't. Honest, Em, I was just—"

"You don't have to explain anything to me, hon. I'm on your side no matter what." She kissed him on his cheek, and whispered in his ear. "It wouldn't have been murder, hon. It wouldn't have killed him. It wasn't such a terrible thing to do. It just would have fixed him up so he'd be able to go any time God decided He wanted him."

"What's gonna happen next, Em?" said Lou hollowly. "What's he gonna do?"

Lou and Emerald stayed fearfully awake almost all night, waiting to see what Gramps was going to do. But not a sound came from the sacred bedroom. At two hours before dawn, the pair dropped off to sleep.

At six o'clock they arose again, for it was time for their generation to eat breakfast in the kitchenette. No one spoke to them. They had twenty minutes in which to eat, but their reflexes were so dulled by the bad night that they had hardly swallowed two mouthfuls of egg-type processed seaweed before it was time to surrender their places to their son's generation.

Then, as was the custom for whomever had been most recently disinherited, they began preparing Gramps' breakfast, which would presently be served to him in bed, on a tray. They tried to be cheerful about it. The toughest part of the job was having to handle the honest-to-God eggs and bacon and oleomargarine on which Gramps spent almost all of the income from his fortune.

"Well," said Emerald, "I'm not going to get all panicky until I'm sure there's something to be panicky about."

"Maybe he doesn't know what it was I busted," said Lou hopefully.

"Probably thinks it was your watch crystal," said Eddie, their son, who was toying apathetically with his buckwheat-type processed sawdust cakes.

"Don't get sarcastic with your father," said Em, "and don't talk with your mouth full, either."

"I'd like to see anybody take a mouthful of this stuff and *not* say something," said Eddie, who was seventy-three. He glanced at the clock. "It's time to take Gramps his breakfast, you know."

"Yeah, it is, isn't it," said Lou weakly. He shrugged. "Let's have the tray, Em."

"We'll both go."

Walking slowly, smiling bravely, they found a large semicircle of long-faced Schwartzes standing around the bedroom door.

Em knocked. "Gramps," she said brightly, "break-fast is rea-dy."

There was no reply, and she knocked again, harder.

The door swung open before her fist. In the middle of the room, the soft, deep, wide, canopied bed, the symbol of the sweet by-and-by to every Schwartz, was empty.

A sense of death, as unfamiliar to the Schwartzes as Zoroastrianism or the causes of the Sepoy Mutiny, stilled every voice and slowed every heart. Awed, the heirs began to search gingerly under the furniture and behind the drapes for all that was mortal of Gramps, father of the race.

But Gramps had left not his earthly husk but a note, which Lou finally found on the dresser, under a paperweight which was a treasured souvenir from the 2000 World's Fair. Unsteadily, Lou read it aloud:

" 'Somebody who I have sheltered and protected and taught the best I know how all these years last night turned on me like a mad dog and diluted my anti-gerasone, or tried to. I am no longer a young man. I can no longer bear the crushing burden of life as I once could. So, after last night's bitter experience, I say goodbye. The cares of this world will soon drop away like a cloak of thorns, and I shall know peace. By the time you find this, I will be gone.' "

"Gosh," said Willy brokenly, "he didn't even get to see how the Five-Hundred-Mile Speedway Race was going to come out."

"Or the World's Series," said Eddie.

"Or whether Mrs. McGarvey got her eyesight back," said Morty.

"There's more," said Lou, and he began reading aloud again: " 'I, Harold D. Schwartz . . . do hereby make, publish and declare this to be my last Will and Testament, hereby revoking any and all former wills and codicils by me at any time heretofore made.' "

"No!" cried Willy. "Not another one!"

" 'I do stipulate,' " read Lou, " 'that all of my property, of whatsoever kind and nature, not be divided, but do devise and bequeath it to be held in common by my issue, without regard for generation, equally, share and share alike.' "

"Issue?" said Emerald.

Lou included the multitude in a sweep of his hand. "It means we all own the whole damn shootin' match."

All eyes turned instantly to the bed.

"Share and share alike?" said Morty.

"Actually," said Willy, who was the oldest person present, "it's just like the old system, where the oldest people head up things with their headquarters in here, and—"

"I like *that!*" said Em. "Lou owns as much of it as you do, and I say it ought to be for the oldest one who's still working. You can snooze around here all day, waiting for your pension check, and poor Lou stumbles in here after work, all tuckered out, and—"

"How about letting somebody who's never had any privacy get a little crack at it?" said Eddie hotly. "Hell, you old people had plenty of privacy back when you were kids. I was born and raised in the middle of the goddam barracks in the hall! How about—"

"Yeah?" said Morty. "Sure, you've all had it pretty tough, and my heart bleeds for you. But try honeymooning in the hall for a real kick."

"Silence!" shouted Willy imperiously. "The next person who opens his mouth spends the next six months by the bathroom. Now clear out of my room. I want to think."

A vase shattered against the wall, inches above his head. In the next moment, a free-for-all was underway, with each couple battling to eject every other couple from the room. Fighting coalitions formed and dissolved with the lightning changes of the tactical situation. Em and Lou were thrown into the hall, where they organized others in the same situation, and stormed back into the room.

After two hours of struggle, with nothing like a decision in sight, the cops broke in.

For the next half-hour, patrol wagons and ambulances hauled away Schwartzes, and then the apartment was still and spacious.

〉〉〉〉〈〈〈〈   〉〉〉〉〈〈〈〈   〉〉〉〉〈〈〈〈

An hour later, films of the last stages of the riot were being televised to 500,000,000 delighted viewers on the Eastern Seaboard.

In the stillness of the three-room Schwartz apartment on the 76th floor of Building 257, the television set had been left on. Once more the air was filled with the cries and grunts and crashes of the fray, coming harmlessly now from the loudspeaker.

The battle also appeared on the screen of the television set in the police station, where the Schwartzes and their captors watched with professional interest.

Em and Lou were in adjacent four-by-eight cells, and were stretched out peacefully on their cots.

"Em—" called Lou through the partition, "you got a washbasin all your own too?"

"Sure. Washbasin, bed, light—the works. Ha! And we thought Gramps' room was something. How long's this been going on?" She held out her hand. "For the first time in forty years, hon, I haven't got the shakes."

"Cross your fingers," said Lou, "the lawyer's going to try to get us a year."

"Gee," said Em dreamily, "I wonder what kind of wires you'd have to pull to get solitary?"

"All right, pipe down," said the turnkey, "or I'll toss the whole kit and caboodle of you right out. And first one who lets on to anybody outside how good jail is ain't never getting back in!"

The prisoners instantly fell silent.

The living room of the Schwartz apartment darkened for a moment, as the riot scenes faded, and then the face of the announcer appeared, like the sun coming from behind a cloud. *"And now, friends,"* he said, *"I have a special message from the makers of anti-gerasone, a message for all you folks over one hundred and fifty. Are you hampered socially by wrinkles, by stiffness of joints and discoloration or loss of hair, all because these things came upon you before anti-gerasone was developed? Well, if you are, you need no longer suffer, need no longer feel different and out of things.*

"After years of research, medical science has now developed super-anti-gerasone! In weeks, yes weeks, you can look, feel, and act as young as your great-great-grandchildren! Wouldn't you pay $5,000 to be indistinguishable from everybody else? Well, you don't have to. Safe, tested super-anti-gerasone costs you only dollars a day. The average cost of regaining all the sparkle and attractiveness of youth is less than fifty dollars.

"Write now for your free trial carton. Just put your name and address on a dollar postcard, and mail it to 'Super,' Box 500,000, Schenectady, N.Y. Have you got that? I'll repeat it. 'Super.' Box . . ." Underlining the announcer's words was the scratching of Gramps' fountain-pen, the one Willy had given him the night before. He had come in a few minutes previous from the Idle Hour Tavern, which commanded a view of Building 257 across the square of asphalt known as the Alden Village Green. He

had called a cleaning woman to come straighten the place up, and had hired the best lawyer in town to get his descendants a conviction. Gramps had then moved the daybed before the television screen so that he could watch from a reclining position. It was something he'd dreamed of doing for years.

"Schen-*ec*-ta-dy," mouthed Gramps. "Got it." His face had changed remarkably. His facial muscles seemed to have relaxed, revealing kindness and equanimity under what had been taut, bad-tempered lines. It was almost as though his trial package of *Super*-anti-gerasone had already arrived. When something amused him on television, he smiled easily, rather than barely managing to lengthen the thin line of his mouth a millimeter. Life was good. He could hardly wait to see what was going to happen next.

SLEEP IT OFF, LADY

Jean Rhys

ONE OCTOBER AFTERNOON Mrs. Baker was having tea with Miss Verney and talking about the proposed broiler factory in the middle of the village where they both lived. Miss Verney, who had not been listening attentively, said, "You know Letty, I've been thinking a great deal about death lately. I hardly ever do, strangely enough."

"No dear," said Mrs. Baker. "It isn't strange at all. It's quite natural. We old people are rather like children, we live in the present as a rule. A merciful dispensation of providence."

"Perhaps," said Miss Verney doubtfully.

Mrs. Baker said "we old people" quite kindly, but could not help knowing that while she herself was only sixty-three and might, with any luck, see many a summer (after many a summer dies the swan, as some man said), Miss Verney, certainly well over seventy, could hardly hope for anything of the sort. Mrs. Baker gripped the arms of her chair. "Many a summer, touch wood and please God," she thought. Then she remarked that it was getting dark so early now and wasn't it extraordinary how time flew.

Miss Verney listened to the sound of the car driving away, went back to her sitting-room and looked out of the window at the flat fields, the apple trees, the lilac tree that wouldn't flower again, not for ten years they told her, because lilacs won't stand being pruned. In the distance there was a rise in the ground—you could hardly call it a hill—and three trees so exactly shaped and spaced that they looked artificial. "It would be rather lovely covered in snow," Miss Verney thought. "The snow, so white, so smooth and in the end so boring. Even the hateful shed wouldn't look so bad." But she'd made up her mind to forget the shed.

Miss Verney had decided that it was an eyesore when she came to live in the cottage. Most of the paint had worn off the once-black galvanized iron. Now it was a greenish color. Part of the roof was loose and flapped noisily in windy weather and a small gate off its hinges leaned up against the entrance. Inside it was astonishingly large, the far end almost dark. "What a waste of

space," Miss Verney thought. "That must come down."
Strange that she hadn't noticed it before.

Nails festooned with rags protruded from the only
wooden rafter. There was a tin bucket with a hole, a huge
dustbin. Nettles flourished in one corner but it was the
opposite corner which disturbed her. Here was piled a
rusty lawnmower, an old chair with a carpet draped over
it, several sacks, and the remains of what had once been
a bundle of hay. She found herself imagining that a fierce
and dangerous animal lived there and called aloud:
"Come out, come out, Shredni Vashtar, the beautiful."
Then rather alarmed at herself she walked away as
quickly as she could.

But she was not unduly worried. The local builder had
done several odd jobs for her when she moved in and she
would speak to him when she saw him next.

"Want the shed down?" said the builder.

"Yes," said Miss Verney. "It's hideous, and it takes up
so much space."

"It's on the large side," the builder said.

"Enormous. Whatever did they use it for?"

"I expect it was the garden shed."

"I don't care what it was," said Miss Verney. "I want
it out of the way."

The builder said that he couldn't manage the next
week, but the Monday after that he'd look in and see
what could be done. Monday came and Miss Verney

waited but he didn't arrive. When this had happened twice she realized that he didn't mean to come and wrote to a firm in the nearest town.

A few days later a cheerful young man knocked at the door, explained who he was and asked if she would let him know exactly what she wanted. Miss Verney, who wasn't feeling at all well, pointed. "I want that pulled down. Can you do it?"

The young man inspected the shed, walked round it, then stood looking at it.

"I want it destroyed," said Miss Verney passionately, "utterly destroyed and carted away. I hate the sight of it."

"Quite a job," he said candidly.

And Miss Verney saw what he meant. Long after she was dead and her cottage had vanished it would survive. The tin bucket and the rusty lawnmower, the pieces of rag fluttering in the wind. All would last for ever.

Eyeing her rather nervously he became businesslike. "I see what you want, and of course we can let you have an estimate of the cost. But you realize that if you pull the shed down you take away from the value of your cottage?"

"Why?" said Miss Verney.

"Well," he said, "very few people would live here without a car. It could be converted into a garage easily or even used as it is. You can decide of course when you have the estimate whether you think it worth the expense and . . . the trouble. Good day."

Left alone, Miss Verney felt so old, lonely and helpless that she began to cry. No builder would tackle that shed, not for any price she could afford. But crying relieved her and she soon felt quite cheerful again. It was ridiculous to brood, she told herself. She quite liked the cottage. One morning she'd wake up and know what to do about the shed, meanwhile she wouldn't look at the thing. She wouldn't think about it.

But it was astonishing how it haunted her dreams. One night she was standing looking at it changing its shape and becoming a very smart, shiny, dark blue coffin picked out in white. It reminded her of a dress she had once worn. A voice behind her said: "That's the laundry."

"Then oughtn't I to put it away?" said Miss Verney in her dream.

"Not just yet. Soon," said the voice so loudly that she woke up.

She had dragged the large dustbin to the entrance and, because it was too heavy for her to lift, had arranged for it to be carried to the gate every week for the dustmen to collect. Every morning she took a small yellow bin from under the sink and emptied it into the large dustbin, quickly, without lingering or looking around. But on one particular morning the usual cold wind had dropped and she stood wondering if a coat of white paint would improve matters. Paint might look a lot worse, besides who could she get to do it? Then she saw a cat, as she thought, walking slowly across the far end. The sun shone through a chink in the wall. It was a large rat. Horrified, she watched it disappear under the old chair, dropped the yellow bin, walked as fast as she was able up the road and knocked at the door of a shabby thatched cottage.

"Oh Tom. There are rats in my shed. I've just seen a huge one. I'm so desperately afraid of them. What shall I do?"

When she left Tom's cottage she was still shaken, but calmer. Tom had assured her that he had an infallible rat poison, arrangements had been made, his wife had supplied a strong cup of tea.

He came that same day to put down the poison, and when afterwards he rapped loudly on the door and shouted: "Everything under control?" she answered quite cheerfully, "Yes, I'm fine and thanks for coming."

As one sunny day followed another she almost forgot how much the rat had frightened her. "It's dead or gone away," she assured herself.

When she saw it again she stood and stared disbelieving. It crossed the shed in the same unhurried way and she watched, not able to move. A huge rat, there was no doubt about it.

This time Miss Verney didn't rush to Tom's cottage to be reassured. She managed to get to the kitchen, still holding the empty yellow pail, slammed the door and locked it. Then she shut and bolted all the windows. This done, she took off her shoes, lay down, pulled the blankets over her head and listened to her hammering heart.

> *I'm the monarch of all I survey.*
> *My right, there is none to dispute.*

That was the way the rat walked.

In the close darkness she must have dozed, for suddenly she was sitting at a desk in the sun copying proverbs into a ruled book: "Evil communications corrupt good manners. Look before you leap. Patience is a virtue, good temper a blessing," all the way up to Z. Z would be something to do with zeal or zealous. But how did they manage about X? What about X?

Thinking this, she slept, then woke, put on the light, took two tuinal tablets and slept again, heavily. When she next opened her eyes it was morning, the unwound bedside clock had stopped, but she guessed the time from the light and hurried into the kitchen waiting for Tom's car to pass. The room was stuffy and airless but she didn't dream of opening the window. When she saw the car approaching she ran out into the road and waved it down. It was as if fear had given her wings and once more she moved lightly and quickly.

"Tom. Tom."

He stopped.

"Oh Tom, the rat's still there. I saw it last evening."

He got down stiffly. Not a young man, but surely, surely, a kind man? "I put down enough stuff to kill a dozen rats," he said. "Let's 'ave a look."

He walked across to the shed. She followed, several yards behind, and watched him rattling the old lawn-mower, kicking the sacks, trampling the hay and nettles.

"No rat 'ere," he said at last.

"Well there was one," she said.

"Not 'ere."

"It was a huge rat," she said.

Tom had round brown eyes, honest eyes, she'd thought. But now they were sly, mocking, even hostile.

"Are you sure it wasn't a pink rat?" he said.

She knew that the bottles in her dustbin were counted and discussed in the village. But Tom, who she liked so much?

"No," she managed to say steadily. "An ordinary color but very large. Don't they say that some rats now don't care about poison? Super rats."

Tom laughed. "Nothing of that sort round 'ere."

She said: "I asked Mr. Slade, who cuts the grass, to clear out the shed and he said he would but I think he's forgotten."

"Mr. Slade is a very busy man," said Tom. "He can't clear out the shed just when you tell him. You've got to wait. Do you expect him to leave his work and waste his time looking for what's not there?"

"No," she said, "of course not. But I think it ought to be done." (She stopped herself from saying: "I can't because I'm afraid.")

"Now you go and make yourself a nice cup of tea," Tom said, speaking in a more friendly voice. "There's no rat in your shed." And he went back to his car.

Miss Verney slumped heavily into the kitchen arm-chair. "He doesn't believe me. I can't stay alone in this place, not with that monster a few yards away. I can't do it." But another cold voice persisted: "Where will you go? With what money? Are you really such a coward as all that?"

After a time Miss Verney got up. She dragged what furniture there was away from the walls so that she would know that nothing lurked in the corners and decided to keep the windows looking onto the shed shut and bolted. The others she opened but only at the top. Then she made a large parcel of all the food that the rat could possibly smell—cheese, bacon, ham, cold meat, practically everything . . . she'd give it to Mrs. Randolph, the cleaning woman, later.

"But no more confidences." Mrs. Randolph would be as sceptical as Tom had been. A nice woman but a gossip, she wouldn't be able to resist telling her cronies about the giant, almost certainly imaginary, rat terrorizing her employer.

Next morning Mrs. Randolph said that a stray dog had upset the large dustbin. She'd had to pick everything up from the floor of the shed. "It wasn't a dog," thought Miss Verney, but she only suggested that two stones on the lid turned the other way up would keep the dog off.

When she saw the size of the stones she nearly said aloud: "I defy any rat to get that lid off."

Miss Verney had always been a careless, not a fussy, woman. Now all that changed. She spent hours every day sweeping, dusting, arranging the cupboards and putting fresh paper into the drawers. She pounced on every speck of dust with a dustpan. She tried to convince herself that as long as she kept her house spotlessly clean the rat would keep to the shed, not to wonder what she would do if, after all, she encountered it.

"I'd collapse," she thought, "that's what I'd do."

After this she'd start with fresh energy, again fearfully sweeping under the bed, behind cupboards. Then feeling too tired to eat, she would beat up an egg in cold milk, add a good deal of whisky and sip it slowly. "I don't need a lot of food now." But her work in the house grew slower and slower, her daily walks shorter and shorter. Finally the walks stopped. "Why should I bother?" As she never answered letters, letters ceased to arrive, and when Tom knocked at the door one day to ask how she was: "Oh I'm quite all right," she said and smiled.

He seemed ill at ease and didn't speak about rats or clearing the shed out. Nor did she.

"Not seen you about lately," he said.

"Oh I go the other way now."

When she shut the door after him she thought: "And I imagined I liked him. How very strange."

"No pain?" the doctor asked.

"It's just an odd feeling," said Miss Verney.

The doctor said nothing. He waited.

"It's as if all my blood was running backwards. It's rather horrible really. And then for a while sometimes I can't move. I mean if I'm holding a cup I have to drop it because there's no life in my arm."

"And how long does this last?"

"Not long. Only a few minutes I suppose. It just seems a long time."

"Does it happen often?"

"Twice lately."

The doctor thought he'd better examine her. Eventually he left the room and came back with a bottle half full of pills. "Take these three times a day—don't forget, it's important. Long before they're finished I'll come and see you. I'm going to give you some injections that may help, but I'll have to send away for those."

As Miss Verney was gathering her things together before leaving the surgery he asked in a casual voice: "Are you on the telephone?"

"No," said Miss Verney, "but I have an arrangement with some people."

"You told me. But those people are some way off, aren't they?"

"I'll get a telephone," said Miss Verney making up her mind. "I'll see about it at once."

"Good. You won't be so lonely."

"I suppose not."

"Don't go moving the furniture about, will you? Don't lift heavy weights. Don't . . ." ("Oh Lord," she thought, "is he going to say 'Don't drink!'—because that's impossible!") . . . "Don't worry," he said.

When Miss Verney left his surgery she felt relieved but tired and she walked very slowly home. It was quite a long walk for she lived in the less prosperous part of the village, near the row of council houses. She had never minded that. She was protected by tall thick hedges and a tree or two. Of course it had taken her some time to get used to the children's loud shrieking and the women who stood outside their doors to gossip. At first they stared at her with curiosity and some disapproval, she couldn't help feeling, but they'd soon found out that she was harmless.

The child Deena, however, was a very different matter.

Most of the village boys were called Jack, Willie, Stan and so on—the girls' first names were more elaborate. Deena's mother had gone one better than anyone else and christened her daughter Undine.

Deena—as everyone called her—was a tall plump girl of about twelve with a pretty, healthy but rather bovine face. She never joined the shrieking games, she never played football with dustbin lids. She apparently spent all her spare time standing at the gate of her mother's house silently, unsmilingly, staring at everyone who passed.

Miss Verney had long ago given up trying to be friendly. So much did the child's cynical eyes depress her that she would cross over the road to avoid her, and sometimes was guilty of the cowardice of making sure Deena wasn't there before setting out.

Now she looked anxiously along the street and was relieved that it was empty. "Of course," she told herself, "it's getting cold. When winter comes they'll all stay indoors."

Not that Deena seemed to mind cold. Only a few days ago, looking out of the window, Miss Verney had seen her standing outside—oblivious of the bitter wind—staring at the front door as though, if she looked hard enough, she could see through the wood and find out what went on in the silent house—what Miss Verney did with herself all day.

>≪≪≪   >≪≪≪   >≪≪≪

One morning soon after her visit to the doctor Miss Verney woke feeling very well and very happy. Also she was not at all certain where she was. She lay luxuriating in the feeling of renewed youth, renewed health, and slowly recognized the various pieces of furniture.

"Of course," she thought when she drew the curtains. "What a funny place to end up in."

The sky was pale blue. There was no wind. Watching the still trees she sang softly to herself: "The day of days." She had always sung "The day of days" on her birthday. Poised between two years—last year, next year —she never felt any age at all. Birthdays were a pause, a rest.

In the midst of slow dressing she remembered the rat for the first time. But that seemed something that had happened long ago. "Thank God I didn't tell anybody else how frightened I was. As soon as they give me a telephone I'll ask Letty Baker to tea. She'll know exactly the sensible thing to do."

Out of habit she ate, swept and dusted but even more slowly than usual and with long pauses, when leaning on the handle of her tall, old-fashioned, carpet sweeper she stared out at the trees. "Goodbye summer. Goodbye goodbye," she hummed. But in spite of sad songs she never lost the certainty of health, of youth.

All at once she noticed, to her surprise, that it was getting dark. "And I haven't emptied the dustbin."

She got to the shed carrying the small yellow plastic pail and saw that the big dustbin wasn't there. For once Mrs. Randolph must have slipped up and left it outside the gate. Indeed it was so.

She first brought in the lid, easy, then turned the heavy bin onto its side and kicked it along. But this was slow. Growing impatient, she picked it up, carried it into the shed and looked for the stones that had defeated the dog, the rat. They too were missing and she realized that Mrs. Randolph, a hefty young woman in a hurry, must have taken out the bin, stones and all. They would be in the road where the dustmen had thrown them. She went to look and there they were.

She picked up the first stone and, astonished at its weight, immediately dropped it. But lifted it again and staggered to the shed, then leaned breathless against the cold wall. After a few minutes she breathed more easily, was less exhausted, and the determination to prove to herself that she was quite well again drove her into the road to pick up the second stone.

After a few steps she felt that she had been walking for a long time, for years, weighed down by an impossible weight, and now her strength was gone and she couldn't any more. Still, she reached the shed, dropped the stone and said: "That's all now, that's the lot. Only the yellow plastic pail to tackle." She'd fix the stones tomorrow. The yellow pail was light, full of paper, eggshells, stale bread. Miss Verney lifted it. . . .

She was sitting on the ground with her back against the dustbin and her legs stretched out, surrounded by torn paper and eggshells. Her skirt had ridden up and there was a slice of stale bread on her bare knee. She felt very cold and it was nearly dark.

"What happened," she thought, "did I faint or something? I must go back to the house."

She tried to get up but it was as if she were glued to the ground. "Wait," she thought. "Don't panic. Breathe deeply. Relax." But when she tried again she was lead. "This has happened before. I'll be all right soon," she told herself. But darkness was coming on very quickly.

Some women passed on the road and she called to them. At first: "Could you please . . . I'm so sorry to trouble you . . ." but the wind had got up and was blowing against her and no one heard. "Help!" she called. Still no one heard.

Tightly buttoned up, carrying string bags, heads in headscarves, they passed and the road was empty.

With her back against the dustbin, shivering with cold, she prayed: "God, don't leave me here. Dear God, let someone come. Let someone come!"

When she opened her eyes she was not at all surprised to see a figure leaning on her gate.

"Deena! Deena!" she called, trying to keep the hysterical relief out of her voice.

Deena advanced cautiously, stood a few yards off and

contemplated Miss Verney lying near the dustbin with an expressionless face.

"Listen Deena," said Miss Verney. "I'm afraid I'm not very well. Will you please ask your mother—your mum —to telephone to the doctor. He'll come I think. And if only she could help me back into the house. I'm very cold. . . ."

Deena said: "It's no good my asking mum. She doesn't like you and she doesn't want to have anything to do with you. She hates stuck-up people. Everybody knows that you shut yourself up to get drunk. People can hear you falling about. 'She ought to take more water with it,' my mum says. Sleep it off, lady," said this horrible child, skipping away.

Miss Verney didn't try to call her back or argue. She knew that it was useless. A numb weak feeling slowly took possession of her. Stronger than cold. Stronger than fear. It was a great unwillingness to do anything more at all—it was almost resignation. Even if someone else came, would she call again for help. Could she? Fighting the cold numbness she made a last tremendous effort to move, at any rate to jerk the bread off her knee, for now her fear of the rat, forgotten all day, began to torment her.

It was impossible.

She strained her eyes to see into the corner where it would certainly appear—the corner with the old chair and carpet, the corner with the bundle of hay. Would it attack at once or would it wait until it was sure that she couldn't move? Sooner or later it would come. So Miss Verney waited in the darkness for the Super Rat.

It was the postman who found her. He had a parcel of books for her and he left them as usual in the passage. But he couldn't help noticing that all the lights were on and all the doors open. Miss Verney was certainly not in the cottage.

"I suppose she's gone out. But so early and such a cold morning?"

Uneasy, he looked back at the gate and saw the bundle of clothes near the shed.

He managed to lift her and got her into the kitchen armchair. There was an open bottle of whisky on the table and he tried to force her to drink some, but her teeth were tightly clenched and the whisky spilled all over her face.

He remembered that there was a telephone in the house where he was to deliver next. He must hurry.

In less time than you'd think, considering it was a remote village, the doctor appeared and shortly afterwards the ambulance.

Miss Verney died that evening in the nearest hospital without recovering consciousness. The doctor said she died of shock and cold. He was treating her for a heart condition, he said.

"Very widespread now—a heart condition."

I USED TO LIVE HERE ONCE

Jean Rhys

SHE WAS STANDING by the river looking at the stepping stones and remembering each one. There was the round unsteady stone, the pointed one, the flat one in the middle—the safe stone where you could stand and look round. The next wasn't so safe for when the river was full the water flowed over it and even when it showed dry it was slippery. But after that it was easy and soon she was standing on the other side.

The road was much wider than it used to be but the work had been done carelessly. The felled trees had not been cleared away and the bushes looked trampled. Yet it was the same road and she walked along feeling extraordinarily happy.

It was a fine day, a blue day. The only thing was that

the sky had a glassy look that she didn't remember. That was the only word she could think of. Glassy. She turned the corner, saw that what had been the old pavé had been taken up, and there too the road was much wider, but it had the same unfinished look.

She came to the worn stone steps that led up to the house and her heart began to beat. The screw pine was gone, so was the mock summer house called the ajoupa, but the clove tree was still there and at the top of the steps the rough lawn stretched away, just as she remembered it. She stopped and looked towards the house that had been added to and painted white. It was strange to see a car standing in front of it.

There were two children under the big mango tree, a boy and a little girl, and she waved to them and called "Hello" but they didn't answer her or turn their heads. Very fair children, as Europeans born in the West Indies so often are: as if the white blood is asserting itself against all odds.

The grass was yellow in the hot sunlight as she walked towards them. When she was quite close she called again, shyly: "Hello." Then, "I used to live here once," she said.

Still they didn't answer. When she said for the third time "Hello" she was quite near them. Her arms went out instinctively with the longing to touch them.

It was the boy who turned. His grey eyes looked

straight into hers. His expression didn't change. He said: "Hasn't it gone cold all of a sudden. D'you notice? Let's go in." "Yes let's," said the girl.

Her arms fell to her sides as she watched them running across the grass to the house. That was the first time she knew.